Incredible
iPhone® Apps
FOR
DUMMIES®

by Bob LeVitus

WILEY

Wiley Publishing, Inc.

Incredible iPhone® Apps For Dummies®

Published by
Wiley Publishing, Inc.
111 River Street
Hoboken, NJ 07030-5774

www.wiley.com

For general information on our other products and services, please contact our Customer Care Department within the U.S. at 877-762-2974, outside the U.S. at 317-572-3993, or fax 317-572-4002.

For technical support, please visit www.wiley.com/techsupport.

Wiley also publishes its books in a variety of electronic formats. Some content that appears in print may not be available in electronic books.

Library of Congress Control Number: 2009943641

ISBN: 978-0-470-60754-1

Manufactured in the United States of America

10 9 8 7 6 5 4 3 2 1

WILEY

About the Author

Bob LeVitus, often referred to as "Dr. Mac," has written or co-written more than 50 popular computer books, including *iPhone For Dummies*, 3rd Edition, *Mac OS X Snow Leopard For Dummies*, and *Dr. Mac: The OS X Files* for Wiley Publishing, Inc.; *Stupid Mac Tricks* and *Dr. Macintosh* for Addison-Wesley; and *The Little iTunes Book* and *The Little iDVD Book* for Peachpit Press. His books have sold more than one million copies worldwide.

Bob has penned the popular "Dr. Mac" column for the *Houston Chronicle* for the past 11 years and has been published in dozens of computer magazines over the past 20 years. His achievements have been documented in major media around the world. (Yes, that was him juggling a keyboard in *USA Today* a few years back!)

Bob is known for his expertise, trademark humorous style, and ability to translate techie jargon into usable and fun advice for regular folks. Bob is also a prolific public speaker, presenting more than 100 Macworld Expo training sessions in the U.S. and abroad, keynote addresses in three countries, and Macintosh training seminars in many U.S. cities. (He also won the Macworld Expo MacJeopardy World Championship three times before retiring his crown.)

Bob is considered one of the world's leading authorities on Mac OS X. From 1989 to 1997, he was a contributing editor/columnist for *MacUser* magazine, writing the "Help Folder," "Beating the System," "Personal Best," and "Game Room" columns at various times.

In his copious spare time, Bob heads up a team of expert technical consultants who do nothing but provide technical help and training to Mac users via telephone, e-mail, and/or their unique Internet-enabled remote control software, which allows the team to see and control your Mac no matter where in the world you may be.

If you're having problems with your Mac, you ought to give them a try. You'll find them at www.boblevitus.com or 408-627-7577.

Prior to giving his life over to computers, Bob spent years at Kresser/Craig/D.I.K. (a Los Angeles advertising agency and marketing consultancy) and its subsidiary, L & J Research. He holds a B.S. in Marketing from California State University.

Cover Credits

Dedication

This book is dedicated to my wife of more than 25 years, the lovely Lisa, who taught me almost everything I know about almost everything I know that's not made by Apple, Inc. And to my children, Allison and Jacob, who love their iPhones almost as much as I love them (the kids, not their iPhones).

Author's Acknowledgments

Extra super special thanks to Bryan Chaffin for pitching in when I needed help with researching and writing, and for being an all around awesome guy I'm proud to call my friend.

Thanks also to super-agent Carole "still Swifty after all these years" Jelen, for deal-making beyond the call of duty yet again. You've represented me for over 20 years; I hope you'll represent me for the next 20 or more.

Big-time thanks to the gang at Wiley: Bob "Is the damn thing done yet?" Woerner, Jodi "The Mellow Mistress of Editorial" Jensen, Andy "Big Boss Man" Cummings, Barry "Still no humorous nickname" Pruett, plus anyone and everyone else at Wiley who was involved in this production.

Thanks also to my family and friends, for putting up with my all-too-lengthy absences during this book's gestation. And thanks to Saccone's Pizza, Rudy's BBQ, Taco Cabana, the Soda-Club System, and HEB for sustenance.

And finally, thanks to you, gentle reader, for buying this book.

Publisher's Acknowledgments

We're proud of this book; please send us your comments at http://dummies.custhelp.com. For other comments, please contact our Customer Care Department within the U.S. at 877-762-2974, outside the U.S. at 317-572-3993, or fax 317-572-4002.

Some of the people who helped bring this book to market include the following:

Acquisitions and Editorial

Project Editor: Jodi Jensen

Executive Editor: Bob Woerner

Copy Editors: Charlotte Kughen, Linda Morris

Editorial Manager: Jodi Jensen

Editorial Assistant: Amanda Graham

Sr. Editorial Assistant: Cherie Case

Composition Services

Project Coordinator: Kristie Rees

Layout and Graphics: Erin Zeltner

Proofreaders: John Greenough, Jessica Kramer, Linda Seifert

Publishing and Editorial for Technology Dummies

Richard Swadley, Vice President and Executive Group Publisher

Andy Cummings, Vice President and Publisher

Mary Bednarek, Executive Acquisitions Director

Mary C. Corder, Editorial Director

Publishing for Consumer Dummies

Diane Graves Steele, Vice President and Publisher

Composition Services

Debbie Stailey, Director of Composition Services

Table of Contents

Introduction

Let me get one thing out of the way right from the get-go. I think you're pretty darn smart for buying a *For Dummies* book. That says to me that you have the confidence and intelligence to know what you don't know. The *For Dummies* franchise is built around the core notion that all of us feel insecure about certain topics when tackling them for the first time, especially when those topics have to do with technology.

And speaking of "Dummies," remember that it's just a word. I don't think you're dumb — quite the opposite! And, for what it's worth, I asked if we could leave "Dummies" out of the title and call it something like, *Incredible iPhone Apps For People Smart Enough to Know They Couldn't Possibly Evaluate Thousands of iPhone Apps and Live to Tell About It.* My editors just laughed. "C'mon, that's the whole point of the name!" they insisted. "And besides, it's shorter our way."

Sigh.

About This Book

This, my 55th technical book, was almost certainly the hardest book I've had to write. Yet I think I had more fun writing it than any of the others. Here's why. . . .

More than 100,000 apps are available in the iTunes App Store today, with thousands more added each week. No single human (or even a rather large *team* of humans) could look at them all, much less give every one of them a thorough workout.

So my first challenge was to narrow the field to a manageable size. I began by looking for apps that had achieved some measure of acclaim, a combination of iTunes Store ranking, positive buzz on the Web, iTunes Store reviews, the opinions of friends and colleagues who matter (you know who you are), the opinions of my family, the opinions of the many enthusiastic iPhone fans at Wiley Publishing, reviews in print, and reviews on the Web. Then I added the thousands of dollars' worth of apps already in my personal collection. When all was said and done, I had way more than 600 apps that were contenders, and I spent several months testing them, taking notes, and capturing screen shots.

My next challenge was figuring out how many categories (chapters) should be included and which ones they should be. This was almost as hard as determining the 600+ contenders. But after much deliberation and consideration, I decided that there would be 16 incredible apps chapters plus 3 bonus "top ten" chapters.

Deciding on the number of apps that would appear in each chapter was easier: I suggested ten and nobody argued, so that was that.

Selecting the 160 most incredible apps (16 chapters × 10 apps) was incredibly difficult, as was deciding where each app belonged. Many apps could just as easily fit in one chapter as another. The Dictionary! app, for example, would be equally at home in the Books, Education, or Reference chapter. So where does it go? The Rock Band app could appear in the Music chapter or the Games chapter. Which is more appropriate? Don't even get me started on Business, Utility, and Productivity apps. It was impossible, so in the end, I just went with my heart.

So if you think I put an app in the wrong chapter, just know that I did the best I could at an impossible task and take some pity on me.

How This Book Is Organized

While we're on the subject of chapters, here's something I imagine you've never heard before: Most books have a beginning, a middle, and an end. Generally, you do well to adhere to that linear structure — unless you're one of those knuckleheads out to ruin it for the rest of us by jumping ahead and revealing that the butler did it.

Fortunately, there is no ending to spoil in a *For Dummies* book. So although you may want to digest this book from start to finish — and I hope you do — I won't penalize you for skipping ahead or jumping around. Having said that, I organized *Incredible iPhone Apps For Dummies* and the contents of each chapter in the order I think makes the most sense — alphabetical.

So the 16 chapters are organized from *A* to *Z:* Books; Business; Education; Entertainment; Finance, Food Cooking and Nutrition; Games; Healthcare and Fitness; Music; Photography; Productivity; Reference; Social Networking; Sports; Travel, Navigation, and Weather; and Utilities.

Each chapter in the book contains five apps, listed alphabetically, each getting two full pages of description and pictures. These five apps are followed by five more apps, also alphabetized, with shorter descriptions. The five apps with the longer descriptions and pictures were selected only because I felt those were the apps that would benefit most from longer descriptions and pictures. The five apps with shorter descriptions and no pictures were the ones I felt I could describe adequately in a paragraph or two.

Please understand that the apps are not ranked in any way within the chapter. Ranking the apps #1 through #10 was more than I could bear; just think of the ten apps in each chapter as more or less equally incredible.

Last, but not least, you'll find three chapters at the end with top-ten lists styled after the chapters found in "The Part of Tens" in a regular *For Dummies* book — think of it as the *For Dummies* answer to David Letterman. The lists presented in Chapters 17 and 18 steer you to my favorite free and paid iPhone apps. If you read this book from cover to cover, you'll already know about the apps I discuss in Chapters 17 and 18 — because they are, after all, my favorites. But I try not to repeat myself. Instead, I explain why each app made the cut and offer some tips or discuss some additional features of each app. The final top-ten list, in Chapter 19, offers my suggestions for some essential iPhone peripherals and accessories you might want to consider adding to your phone.

Conventions Used in This Book

First, I want to tell you how I go about my business. *Incredible iPhone Apps For Dummies* makes generous use of bullet lists and pictures. And all Web and e-mail addresses are shown in a special monofont typeface, `like this`.

There are no links to the App Store because they're long and easy to mistype. Rather, we took great pains to ensure that all app names are properly spelled, so you should have no trouble finding them using the App Store's search engine.

I've listed prices for each app, and these prices were accurate at the time this book was printed. That said, developers change App prices regularly, so the price you see in the book may not be the same as the price you see in the App Store. Rest assured, it was right when this book went to press and if it's not right anymore, please blame (or thank) the developer.

Another thing: I use *iPhone* throughout the book, but in most cases what I really mean is *iPhone and iPod touch.* Almost all iPhone apps also run on the iPod touch, but I didn't want to have to type the longer form thousands of times. So when you see the word *iPhone,* replace it in your mind with *iPhone and iPod touch.*

Icons Used in This Book

Little round pictures (icons) appear in the left margins throughout this book. Consider these icons miniature road signs, telling you something extra about the topic at hand or hammering a point home.

Here's what the three icons used in this book look like and mean.

These are the juicy morsels, shortcuts, and recommendations that might make the task at hand faster or easier.

This icon emphasizes the stuff I think you ought to retain. You may even jot down a note to yourself in the iPhone.

You wouldn't intentionally run a stop sign, would you? In the same fashion, ignoring warnings may be hazardous to your iPhone and (by extension) your wallet. There, you now know how these warning icons work: You have just received your very first warning!

A Note about Project Gutenberg

Most books published in the United States prior to 1923 are considered to be in the *public domain.* This means they are free of copyright and that anyone can print them, distribute them electronically, or even charge money for them. Project Gutenberg (www.gutenberg.org) is the first and largest single collection of free electronic books (*e-books*) on the Web today with more than 30,000 free books. I mention Project Gutenberg and its plethora of titles several times in these pages. Now you know what I'm referring to.

Where to Go from Here

Why straight to Chapter 1, of course (without passing Go). But first, there is one more thing.

I didn't write this book for myself. I wrote it for you — and I would love to hear how it worked for you. So please send me your thoughts, platitudes, likes and dislikes, and any other comments. You can send snail-mail in care of Wiley, but it takes a long time to reach me that way, and I just don't have time to respond to 99.9% of it. If you want a response, your best bet is to send e-mail to me directly at incredibleiphoneapps@boblevitus.com. I appreciate your feedback, and I try to respond to all reasonably polite e-mail within a few days.

Last, but not least, let me make you an offer you can't refuse: If you know of an app you think should appear in the next edition of this book, please send me an e-mail message explaining why you think so and the chapter you think it belongs in. If I like the app enough to include it in the next edition of this book, I'll not only thank you in the acknowledgements section, I'll also send you a free autographed copy of the book. You've got to love that!

Okay, that's all I've got for now. Go — enjoy the book!

1 Books

Audiobook Player
$0.99 US

My wife and I have always enjoyed listening to audiobooks in our cars. First we listened to cassette tapes; then we listened to CDs; and now we use our iPhones. Until recently, we spent $10 to $20 each month on audiobooks from Audible.com (www.audible.com). Then we discovered the fantastic Audiobook Player app from Alex Sokirynsky. With Audiobook Player, we can easily find, download, and listen to more than 2,300 free books.

Audiobook Player's iTunes App Store description claims that it's "the best way to enjoy streaming or offline playback of free audio books on the iPhone and iPod touch." Audiobook Player is definitely the easiest way to find and download free audio books with its several ways to browse or search for titles that interest you, as shown in the figure on the left.

I'd be remiss, gentle reader, if I didn't at least mention that Audiobook Player gets almost all of its content from Librivox (http://librivox.org), a non-commercial, non-profit, ad-free project run by volunteers. Librivox donates all of its volunteer-made recordings to the public domain.

If you don't want to pay 99¢ or you don't care for this app, you can visit the Librivox Web site, download all the audiobooks you like, and import them into iTunes. Audiobook Player just makes it easier to find and manage your audiobook library because you can download new titles right to your iPhone so that you can listen to them immediately. Audiobook Player even breaks the files into chapters.

Best features

One of the best things about Audiobook Player is that — unlike the audiobooks you purchase from Audible.com — you can download free audiobooks one chapter at a time, as shown in the figure on the right, which helps you conserve storage space on your iPhone.

Another nice feature of Audiobook Player is that you can download new titles or chapters over any of your iPhone's three wireless networks — Wi-Fi, 3G, or EDGE.

Finally, there's also a free version called Audiobook Player - FREE, which is the same as the paid version, but you're limited to one book at a time.

Worst features

Although the 2,300 free books include classics in the public domain, such as *The Adventures of Tom Sawyer, Aesop's Fables, Beyond Good and Evil, The Count of Monte Cristo, The Curious Case of Benjamin Button, Pride and Prejudice, Robinson Crusoe,* and *A Tale of Two Cities,* there are few (if any) audiobooks written during *our* lifetimes. This isn't the app's fault, but I still consider it a shortcoming.

If you're looking for current bestsellers or more contemporary fare, the iTunes Store's Audiobook section has a pretty good selection. Keep in mind that the same audiobook you find in the iTunes store often costs less at www.audible.com. You might also check out the AudibleListener Gold plan. My wife and I pay just $14.95 per month for one audiobook a month, even if the audiobook's list price is substantially higher (as most of them are).

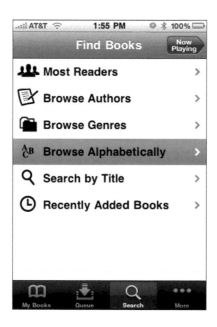

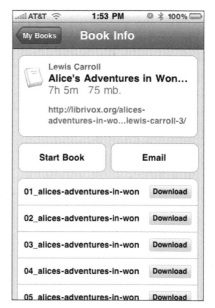

Classics2Go Collection
$0.99 US

Classics2Go is one of the myriad apps you'll find in the App Store that offers a selection of books that are in the public domain. This one includes more than 50 classic books, is easy on the eyes, and offers a couple of unique features. Although I haven't tried every classic book app in the iTunes Store, I've spent at least $20 on the ones that look the most promising. After much deliberation, I've concluded that the Classics2Go Collection is the one I like best.

The Classic2Go library includes more than 50 classics such as *The Illiad* and *The Odyssey, The Adventures of Sherlock Holmes, Call of the Wild, Hound of the Baskervilles, Siddhartha, Dracula, Dr. Jekyll and Mr. Hyde, The Curious Case of Benjamin Button, Frankenstein,* and dozens more.

One thing that makes this app unique is that several of the books — including *Alice in Wonderland, A Christmas Carol,* and *Flatland* — feature illustrations, as shown in the figure on the left.

Some apps that are similar to Classics2Go have poorly formatted text with strange line endings and weird page breaks, or they feature ugly typography in unattractive fonts. The books in Classics2Go Collection, though, are nicely formatted and typeset as shown in the figure on the right.

Best features

What I like best about Classics2Go Collection is the elegant typography, thoughtful page layout, and clear, readable text. It's obvious that the developers didn't just copy and paste the raw Project Gutenberg text into the app (see the Introduction to this book for info on Project Gutenberg). The upshot is that text in this app looks better than the text in most of the other "reading" apps I've tested.

Another plus is the quantity and quality of the available titles. You've got to love getting more than 50 of the world's greatest books for less than a buck. Although some of these books are available in other classic book apps, the Classics2Go Collection contains many more books that I'm likely to read and enjoy.

A free version of the app is available. It's called Classics2GoLite Collection and has the same features as the paid version but includes only six books: *The Adventures of Sherlock Holmes, Alice in*

Wonderland, A Christmas Carol, The Curious Case of Benjamin Button, Pride and Prejudice, and *Romeo and Juliet.* So before you plunk down the whopping 99¢ for Classics2 Go Collection, you can check out the interface to make sure you like it.

Worst features

The biggest problem I have with Classics2Go Collection is that you can't select a different font size. I usually find myself wishing I could make text bigger on my iPhone, but in the case of Classics2Go Collection, I'd like to make it a little smaller so that I wouldn't have to turn the page as often. Other than this small complaint, I've found that Classics2Go Collection provides a most pleasant reading experience with nice touches you won't find in other apps.

If you don't want to pay for a public domain book collection, you can download from Project Gutenberg most (if not all) the books any of the similar apps offer. Save them as Microsoft Word, PDF, or plain text files, or send them to yourself in the body of an e-mail message (or messages) so that you can view them on your iPhone without purchasing additional software.

Although downloading from Project Gutenberg may save you a buck or two, you'll miss out on all the cool goodies Classics2Go (and similar apps) offers, such as bookmarks, optimized typography, tables of contents, and illustrations.

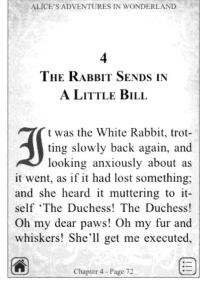

Comics
Free

The Comics app is a front-end to the largest comic book library online, offers a ton of free content, and provides a well-designed interface that makes viewing comics on a small screen more pleasant than other comic book reader apps.

Comics is actually three different apps rolled into one. First and foremost, it's a fantastic way of reading comic books on a 3.5-inch touch screen. It's also a comic book store with hundreds of individual comics from dozens of different publishers, including Arcana Comics, Devil's Due, Digital Webbing, Red 5, Zenescope, and many others. Last but not least, it's a great way to organize the comics you own on your iPhone so you can find the one you want quickly and easily.

Let's start with the viewer. Wired.com says Comics, "solves the problem of reading comics on the small screen," and I have to agree. The comics are presented in Comixology's patent-pending Guided View, which keeps the page intact as its creators intended. It "guides" you from panel to panel with beautiful transition animations, panning across frames and offering dramatic pull-backs that enhance the viewing experience, as shown in the figure on the left (which is from Atomic Robo #1, one of many free comics available through the Comics app's built-in comic book store).

In all fairness, comic book purists like my friend Andy Ihnatko don't much care for enhancements such as Guided View. In fact, he recently wrote an article for the *Chicago Sun-Times* in which he expressed his distain for such frippery: "Even when 'motion comics' are done with great expense and care (such as Marvel's recent 'Spider-Woman' offering) the overall effect is sock-puppety at best."

Some people say opinions are like noses (or other body parts not normally mentioned in a G-rated book such as this) because everybody has one. I'm sorry, Andy, but in my humble opinion the animations are innovative and not at all "sock-puppety." In fact, I'd go so far as to say that I think Comixology's Guided View looks much better than the other comic book reader apps that abruptly jump from panel to panel. Call me ignorant or unsophisticated or whatever you like, but I say Guided View is very cool and is a reason to love this app.

The free Comics app includes more than 65 free comics, including a good exclusive weekly series — Box 13. If you want more comics, use the Comics app's excellent in-app comic store (see the figure on the right), which offers hundreds of comics and series and generally lets you download for free the first issue in a series to see if you like it enough to buy subsequent issues. Most of the comics in the store cost 99¢ to $1.99.

New releases are available every Wednesday, so visit the store often to check out the latest and greatest offerings. And speaking of new offerings, the latest version of Comics, which came out while I was writing this chapter, offers push notifications so you'll never miss new issues of your favorite comic book series.

Finally, both the store and your personal comic collection are well-organized and easy to use.

Best features

Comics provides a fantastic viewing experience — immersive, enjoyable, and more cinematic than you expect from a comic book.

Worst features

Comics offers lots of different comics, but I've never heard of many of them. Although that's not necessarily a bad thing, I'd love to see more comics from the big guys (such as Marvel and DC Comics) available in the Comics store.

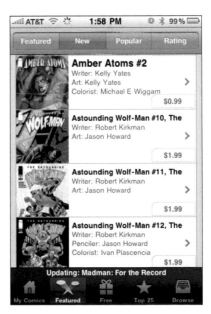

Kindle for iPhone
Free

Amazon.com's free Kindle app lets you shop for hundreds of thousands of eBooks, newspapers, and magazines at Amazon.com and read them at your leisure on your iPhone.

Before I tell you about the Kindle app, though, you need to know about the Kindle device that it emulates.

The Kindle is Amazon.com's $250+ wireless handheld reading device (see the figure on the left), which lets you shop for, buy, and read Kindle books, magazines, and newspapers on its black-and-white screen.

The Kindle app for the iPhone (see the figure on the right) does more or less the same things as a Kindle, but on your iPhone instead of on a separate, bulky, expensive, single-purpose device.

Amazon's Kindle store offers more than 350,000 books, as well as newspapers, magazines, and blogs at prices well below their printed counterparts. You can read the books, newspapers, and magazines you buy on the Kindle device or on your iPhone with the free Kindle app.

The best thing about reading anything on either the Kindle device or with the Kindle app is that prices for the electronic versions of books are almost always a lot less than the printed versions. For example, some of the best deals are on *The New York Times* Best Sellers, which generally cost just $9.99 for the Kindle version. At press time, examples of best-selling titles include Dan Brown's *The Lost Symbol* ($29.95 in print; 67% saved); James Patterson and Richard DiLallo's *Alex Cross's Trial* ($27.99 in print; 64% saved); E. L. Doctorow's *Homer & Langley: A Novel* ($26 in print; 62% saved); and Jon Krakauer's *Where Men Win Glory: The Odyssey of Pat Tillman* ($27.95 in print; 64% saved). Magazines and newspaper subscriptions are less expensive than their hard copy counterparts, too. For example, *The New York Times* Kindle Edition costs $13.99 per month (vs. $45–$60 per month depending on where you live), and many magazines are less than $2 per month.

Another unique feature of both the Kindle device and the Kindle app for the iPhone is that you can read the beginning of any book free before you buy it.

How does the free Kindle iPhone app stack up to the $250 Kindle device? Glad you asked! The Kindle has a bigger screen than your iPhone and includes a physical keyboard. Unlike your iPhone, the Kindle has a black-and-white screen and doesn't include e-mail, maps, a camera, SMS or MMS messaging, a music player, or a video player. And, of course, you can't install iPhone apps on it.

The Kindle iPhone app lets you read in portrait or landscape mode, choose the text size, choose background and text colors, add bookmarks, and zoom in and out at will. You can also create notes that are backed up automatically, as well as synchronized with your Kindle device (if you happen to own one in addition to owning the Kindle iPhone app).

To be perfectly fair, the Kindle iPhone app lacks some of the Kindle device's features, such as a battery that lasts for days, text-to-speech, full-text search, and a highlighter.

That said, do you really want to pay $250 to lug around a device four or five times larger than your iPhone just to read books and newspapers on a bigger black-and-white screen?

I thought not.

Best features

The best thing about the Kindle app is that the Kindle store has a huge selection of titles, and you can carry almost anything you care to read in your pocket without spending $250 on a separate electronic device.

Worst features

You can't buy books from within the app. It's awkward to shop for and purchase books using a Web browser, and it's especially awkward to do so with Safari on your iPhone's 3.5-inch screen. Lastly, as I mentioned earlier, the iPhone app lacks a search function or highlighter.

Photo courtesy of Amazon.com

Stanza

Free

Stanza is another free eBook reader with more and better features than the Kindle app but a significantly smaller selection of titles.

Unlike the Kindle, there's not a $250 handheld Stanza device, but I suspect most of you won't care.

Stanza has all the features that are missing from the Kindle app and more. Some of Stanza's niceties include almost infinite control over page layout, so you can specify not only font size but also margins, line and paragraph spacing, indentation, page color, and more. Being able to adjust layout settings makes a huge difference, especially if you read in a variety of places with different types of lighting.

You can look up words using the built-in dictionary and jot down annotations, as you can see in the figure on the left.

Plus, you can search for a word or phrase in any book, sort your library by title or author, or even create custom collections within your library. If you're a fan of the Cover Flow view found in iTunes and Mac OS X Leopard and Snow Leopard, you'll be pleased to know that you can browse your Stanza library in a Cover Flow–like view. And, although this is kind of silly, if you don't like the cover that came with a book, you can replace it with other artwork using Stanza's Cover Lookup feature.

You can set multiple bookmarks in each book, and if you leave the app for any reason — a phone call, text message, or just because your eyes are tired — Stanza remembers where you left off and takes you back to that page the next time you launch the app.

If you read in multiple languages, you'll be pleased to know that the Stanza app includes built-in support for English, French, German, Italian, Spanish, Chinese, Japanese, Russian, Danish, Portuguese, and Swedish.

Best of all, Stanza has a fabulous built-in catalog so you can download free content and purchase contemporary books without leaving the app, which is something you can't do with the Kindle app.

With the Kindle, you're limited to content you get at the Kindle Store on Amazon.com. Stanza offers titles from multiple sources, including Random House Free Library, Harlequin Books, and all 25,000+ books from Project Gutenberg, some of which are shown in the figure on the right.

Some of the available authors include Stephanie Meyer (*Twilight*), Dan Brown (*The DaVinci Code*), Malcom Gladwell, (*Blink*), Barack Obama

(*The Audacity of Hope*), Stephen King (too many titles to name), and James Patterson (ditto).

Stanza offers access to a lot of free books, probably more than any other app I've tested, including most (if not all) of the titles found in Classics2Go Collection, as well as other titles from authors such as Edgar Allen Poe, Oscar Wilde, Sir Arthur Conan Doyle, and P. G. Wodehouse.

The Stanza catalog is easy to use and makes finding titles easy to do. You can browse by subject, language, or author, or you can use Stanza's excellent search mechanism.

This app has been lauded by *TIME* magazine (Top 11 iPhone Apps), *PC Magazine* (Editor's Choice), *Wired* (10 Most Awesome iPhone Apps), and BestAppEver.com. Because Stanza is free, you have no excuse not to give it a try.

Best features

I love having complete control over the way my pages look. I wish every app I use to read anything had this feature. I also like all the thoughtful touches such as search, built-in dictionary, and instant annotation.

Worst features

The biggest drawback to this app is its smaller selection of titles (compared to Kindle).

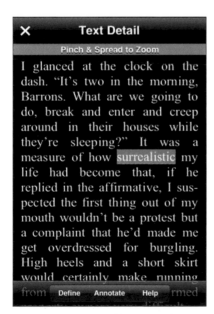
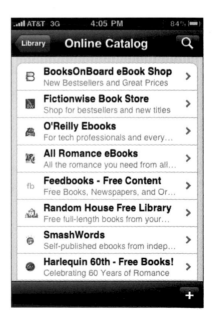

IVerse Comics
Free

IVerse Comics is another comic book reader and store that lets you download both free and inexpensive issues of comic books. Like the Comics app, it has an integrated comic book viewer and is free.

IVerse Comics isn't as elegant as the Comics app. In portrait mode you see a full comic book page at once. To see panels at a readable size, though, you have to flip your phone into landscape mode, which feels clunky compared to Guided View in Comics.

On the other hand, IVerse Comics offers titles not available in the Comics app, including *Archie* comics, Dean Koontz graphic novels, and the excellent *Dynamo 5* series.

Grimm's Fairy Tales by Jacob & Wilhelm Grimm
Free

I've always preferred the darker Grimm versions of fairy tale classics such as *Sleeping Beauty* and *Snow White* to the sanitized Disney renditions, so I was tickled to discover this app.

In addition to more than 200 stories, this free app has pretty much every feature you could ask for and then some. You can choose the typeface, font size, text color, and paper color. The unique AutoScroll feature, which causes the text to scroll up the screen, much like a teleprompter, is way cool. It takes a few minutes to get the hang of using AutoScroll, but after you do, you'll wish every app offered it.

Holy Bible
Free

The Holy Bible app includes six complete translations of the Holy Bible. If that's not enough, with a couple of taps you can download more than a dozen additional translations, including the World English Bible, American Standard Version, and even the Bible in Basic English.

The presentation is slick and professional and includes useful features such as search, notes, bookmarks, and more. I like the way you can drag your finger up or down the right side of the screen to jump to a specific verse.

Unlike most apps, you won't have to wish that the Holy Bible app had AutoScroll because it does.

Self Help Classics
$0.99 US

They say that if something sounds too good to be true it usually is. With the complete text of 16 self-help books for less than a buck, Self Help Classics isn't one of those things. It's good and it's true.

The titles include *Think and Grow Rich* by Napoleon Hill, *The Master Key System* by Charles F. Haanel, *The Art of Public Speaking* by Dale Carnegie and Joseph Berg Esenwein, plus the autobiography of Andrew Carnegie, America's first self-made billionaire.

Then there's the app itself, which is nicely designed and has bookmarks, font size control, navigation shortcut buttons, and (yea!) AutoScroll. Furthermore, the text is nicely set and easy to read.

Shakespeare
Free

If you're a fan of the Bard you'll love this free app, which includes the full texts of 40 plays, all 6 poems, all 154 sonnets, and a searchable concordance.

Produced in part by PlayShakespeare.com, which is known as "the ultimate free Shakespeare resource," the works in this app are drawn from the First Folio of 1623 (and Quartos where applicable) and the Globe Edition of 1866, which have been re-edited and updated to reflect the editorial standards of PlayShakespeare.com's scholarly team.

Finally, this is one of the few apps that has a landscape reading option that hides all the buttons and controls when you turn your iPhone sideways. Yea!

2 Business

Business Card Reader
$5.99 US

Business Card Reader does just what its name implies — takes pictures of business cards and then uses text recognition to convert them into editable text in the appropriate fields of the iPhone's Contacts app.

This app is slick, but before you get too excited you should know that you need an iPhone 3GS to shoot a close-up of a business card that's good enough for Business Card Reader to translate accurately. That said, if you have a first- or second-generation iPhone, you may not be completely out of luck. Griffin Technology makes a polycarbonate case called Clarifi (discussed in Chapter 19) that includes a built-in close-up lens that lets you use Business Card Reader with any iPhone.

Using Business Card Reader couldn't be easier. To capture the information from a business card you tap either the Take Photo button or the Select Picture button. The card is scanned, as shown in the figure on the left. When the scanning is finished, the New Contact screen appears, as shown in the figure on the right.

At this point you can

- ✔ (Optional) Edit the information
- ✔ Tap the Done button to add the information to the iPhone's Contacts app as a new contact
- ✔ Tap the Merge with Existing Contact button to merge the information with a contact that's already in your Contacts list
- ✔ Tap Cancel to throw the info away and not use it at all
- ✔ Tap LinkedIn Lookup to look up the person at www.linkedin.com
- ✔ Tap View Recognized Info as Plain Text to see all the words the OCR (Optical Character Recognition) technology translated on a single screen with no fields

I'd be remiss if I let you believe that every card you scan is recognized as flawlessly as the one shown. (By the way, I purposely blurred the person's name and company to protect the innocent.) In this case, Business Card Reader made just one mistake: It read *Publie* instead of *Public,* as you can see in the figure on the right. The rest of the text — phone number, company name, address, and so on — was recognized with 100% accuracy.

The card I used for this demo worked excellently with OCR. The text is extremely clear; the background is plain white; the items are logically grouped and reasonably spaced.

Business Card Reader has a much tougher time with stylishly designed cards that have busy multi-colored backgrounds, text in decorative fonts, or light colored text against a dark background. To its credit, the app was 70 to 80 percent accurate, even on cards with all three of the aforementioned issues.

For the best results, make sure you have plenty of light when you photograph the card.

Best features

Business Card Reader can save you a lot of typing. And it gives you something to do on the plane ride home from a conference where you've collected a lot of business cards.

Worst features

Business Card Reader produces mediocre results if the card's design is too artistic.

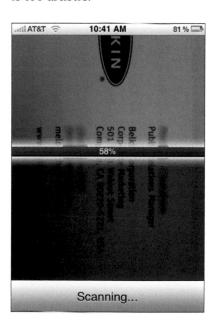
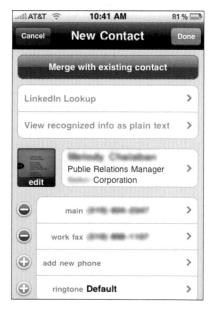

Convertbot
$0.99 US

There is no shortage of iPhone apps that perform unit conversion, such as centimeters to inches, Euros to U.S. dollars, gallons to liters, Fahrenheit to Celsius, and such. I found dozens upon dozens of them while researching this chapter; by the time you read this chapter there will surely be dozens upon dozens more. Although I didn't test every single conversion app, I did test enough to know that if you're only going to have one conversion utility on your iPhone, Convertbot is the one you want.

I have three reasons for concluding that Convertbot is the crème de la crème of unit converters:

1. It has a beautiful and functional user interface, which you can see in both figures.

2. It offers a massive number of unit categories and types.

3. It offers myriad options for customization.

Let's start with examining Convertbot's interface, which is as easy to use as it is beautiful. After picking a category, I select the type of units I want to convert by tapping their names on the unit wheel. In the figure on the left, I'm converting inches to feet and inches. I used the Convertbot numeric keypad (not shown) to specify 91 inches as the From value, and the converted To value (7 feet 7 inches) instantly appears below it.

Convertbot supports more than 440 different kinds of units in 19 separate categories. For example, it can convert between more than 100 different currencies (such as Gold, Silver, Platinum, and Aluminum ounces, as well as the currencies of most civilized nations), nearly 50 different measures of volume (such as bushel, dram, dry pint, and teaspoon), and 40 different measures of length (such as mil, nautical mile, smoot, and league). Convertbot also handles hundreds of other unit types in 16 other categories that include mass, power, fuel, speed, area, data rate, and data size. There are, in fact, so many different types of units that I discovered dozens of them I'd never heard of. For example, do you know what a gigapascal, becquerel, didot, kanejaku, or tsubo measure is? I didn't, but I do now (they measure pressure, radioactivity, typography, length, and area, respectively).

Finally, you can disable categories you don't need (Angle, Force, and Fuel in the figure on the right) and enable the units you do need within each category. In the figure on the right, 10 of 18 units for Area; 9 of 138 for Currency; 17 of 38 for Data Rate; and 10 of 22 for Data Size have been enabled. As you may expect, limiting the choices makes it much quicker and easier to find and use the categories and units you need.

Other niceties of Convertbot include the capability to update all currency values when you launch the app and have an Internet connection. There's also an optional calculator in which you can specify up to 15 places in your calculations.

Convertbot is easy to use, looks great, lets you tailor its capabilities to your actual needs, and costs a lot less than a gallon of milk (which equals 3.785412 liters or 8 pints or 16 cups or 128 fluid ounces or. . .). If you ever need to convert units of measure, you need Convertbot.

Best features

Convertbot is comprehensive, easy to use, and offers a beautiful and extremely customizable interface, yet it costs less than a buck.

Worst features

Convertbot can tell you how many teaspoons are in a tablespoon, but it can't cook dinner for you. In other words, I can't think of a single feature that's "bad," much less one that's the "worst."

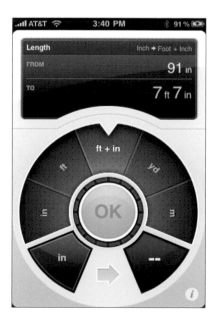

GetPaid!
$4.99 US

GetPaid tracks the time you spend on each job and instantly generates an invoice in either PDF or HTML format. The app's user interface is designed to be easy to use on the job, and it allows you to enter information quickly and painlessly.

In my other life, I'm a computer consultant, technician, and trainer, and I still make house calls. Before I got this app, I often forgot to track when I started and ended a job. In order to not overbill my clients, I often billed them for less time than I had actually spent working on the job. Because I usually sent invoices from my office, I also sometimes entirely forgot to bill a client. I had no organized system to keep track of my hours or earnings. Even worse, I didn't have any formal system for tracking invoices, much less which ones had or had not been paid.

Now I use GetPaid to do all of these things and more. It's so easy to use that I never feel like I'm taking away valuable time from the job.

If a client is in my iPhone Contacts list, with a couple of taps I can add the client to GetPaid. And, of course, I can add new clients manually. Keeping track of the time I spend on each job takes only a few taps. Generating an invoice is a piece of cake and requires only a few more taps (see the figure on the left). After creating an invoice, I can tap the Email button to e-mail the invoice as a PDF or HTML file right from my iPhone, or I can use GetPaid's built-in Wi-Fi–based export mechanism to copy invoices to my computer for printing.

GetPaid is not only quick and easy to use; it's also quite flexible. For example, charging different rates for different services is not a problem, which is great because I charge a different rate for repair services than I do for training. GetPaid also keeps track of multiple sessions with the same client so that I can easily invoice for the total.

Other niceties include built-in passcode protection for the app, data backup and restore, job data exporting (as a .CSV file that you can import to any spreadsheet or database), previews of finished invoices, time-rounding options, plus a calculator, currency converter, and support for international currencies.

The other thing I really like about GetPaid is that I can view paid and unpaid invoices as a pie chart (as shown in the figure on the right) or line graph, which allows me to instantly see my earnings for the past week, month, three months, six months, or year.

Finally, I like that the developers ask for feedback on the app and ask users to e-mail them requests for additional timesheet and invoice templates. The developers say they will "find ways to build it."

If you're a freelancer, mobile professional, temp, consultant, contractor, or anyone else who needs to track your time to get paid, I've yet to find an easier, faster method than the GetPaid app.

Best features

GetPaid makes it really fast and easy to track time spent on jobs, generate invoices, and track the payment of those invoices. Every part of the app is designed for speed, and it's so simple to use you'll probably never need to look at the comprehensive online help.

Worst features

For some unfathomable reason, you can't preview invoices in landscape mode, which makes it harder than it should be to check over an invoice before you send it.

 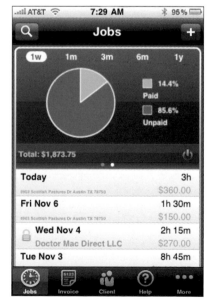

Jaadu VNC

$24.99 US

Jaadu VNC is one of the coolest and most useful apps I have on my iPhone, and by far it's the best app I've tested for remotely controlling my home or office computer. Jaadu VNC can remotely control computers running Mac, Windows, Linux, and AMX touch screen operating systems.

If you've never used a VNC (which stands for Virtual Network Computing) program to control your computer remotely, here's how VNC, also known as *screen sharing,* works. In a nutshell, VNC lets you see a computer's screen and control its mouse and keyboard from another computer — or, in this case, your iPhone — in another location. To prepare a computer for remote control, you first install software called a *VNC server.* For Jaadu VNC, you can download the server software free from the Jaadu Web site. As long as the computer has an Internet connection and is running VNC server software, you can use a username and password to connect to and control the computer from a VNC client app using any computer or iPhone anywhere in the world.

If you've never tried remote control computing, it's a fabulous tool that can be a real lifesaver. VNC has saved my bacon more times than I care to remember. For example, I can log into my office computer from wherever I happen to be to look at the e-mail in my Inbox, as shown in the figure on the left. If there's an urgent message in my Inbox, I can forward it to my iPhone and deal with it from there, or I can reply to the message from my office computer by typing on my iPhone. When I grocery shop, I use Jaadu VNC to look up a recipe on my home computer so that I can be sure to get every ingredient I need. Finally, if I'm away from home and someone calls and says they desperately need a document that's on my Mac, I can use Jaadu VNC to e-mail the person a copy of the document, even if I happen to be on the other side of the world at the time.

Jaadu VNC has full keyboard support, so you can use it to type in any app that's running on your remote computer. It also supports modifier keys such as those shown left to right near the top of the figure on the right: Shift, Control, ⌘, and Option, as well as shortcut buttons for common activities such as quit (an application), close (a window), switch (applications), select all, cut, copy, and paste, which are also shown in the figure on the right.

I've tried several similar but less-expensive VNC client apps that claim to do what Jaadu VNC does, but not a single one has worked nearly as well or as reliably.

Best features

Jaadu VNC lets me be at my computer even when I'm thousands of miles away from it. No matter what emergency crops up, if there's something I need from my home or office Mac, Jaadu VNC gives me a way to access what I need from wherever I happen to be. This app may seem expensive, but to me, it's worth every cent.

Worst features

I use two displays at home, but Jaadu VNC can only access the main one (the one with the menu bar). Consequently, I have to make sure that I don't leave windows or icons on the secondary display if I think I might need to use them via Jaadu VNC.

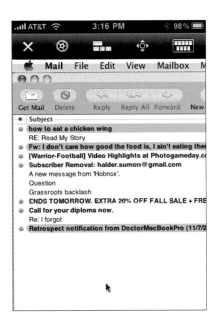
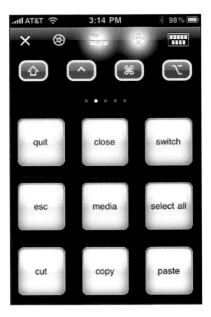

Presenter Pro
$1.99 US

Presenter Pro is a training app that offers superb guidance for anyone who needs to give a presentation to an audience. Regardless of the content of the presentation, the software used, the projection equipment, or the size of the room or audience, Presenter Pro is chock-full of terrific advice and tips to help you convey your message memorably and effectively.

Using a combination of text, photos, audio and video clips, real-world examples, pop-up tips, thought-provoking exercises, and useful quizzes, Presenter Pro conveys a plethora of information without being preachy or boring. I have a short attention span, so I really appreciate that the app stays on topic and uses a variety of media to keep things interesting.

Here's how Presenter Pro works. The main screen has six buttons: Structure, Visuals, Words, Voice, Gestures, and Rate Me, as shown in the figure on the left. Tapping any of the first five buttons reveals a long list of short subtopics. For example, if you tap Words, you see entries that include Affirmative Words, Avoid Apologies, Condescension, and Words for Humans. Tapping a subtopic reveals a textual description that may also include photos, drawings (as shown in the figure on the right), or audio and video clips.

The sixth button, Rate Me, has two possible uses. Using a scale from one to ten, you can rate other presenters or have someone else rate your presentation in areas such as captivating opening, supportive visuals, expressive voice, audience rapport, and memorable ending. You can then save the ratings or e-mail them to someone with a couple additional taps.

In addition to the main screen, there are four buttons at the bottom of the screen: Quiz, Videos, Checklist, and Help. Quiz offers a test with approximately ten questions in each of the main categories — structure, visuals, words, voice, and gestures. Videos provides instant access to the video clips sprinkled throughout the rest of the app. Checklist lets you swipe your finger across a paragraph you want to remember to instantly copy the information to the checklist. I use the checklist to gather all the things I consider most important so that I can read them just before I hit the stage. Help includes a quick overview of the app's components and a brief description of how to use each one.

Another nice touch in Presenter Pro is the "tip shaker" option, which can display a quick tip when you give your iPhone a little shake.

I've delivered hundreds of presentations to audiences of all sizes in dozens of countries. I'm not trying to sound smug, but I have a lot of experience presenting information to crowds, and I think I've become pretty good at it over the years. Even so, I looked at every screen in this app before I put together my most recent presentation (to the Chicago Apple User Group), and I am certain my show was noticeably improved by it.

If you don't present often, Presenter Pro can help you improve your delivery, increase your confidence, and avoid mistakes. But even if delivering presentations is your bread and butter, I'm convinced you'll find a lot of useful information in this app.

Best features

Presenter Pro is chock-full of useful information to help you improve your presentation skills. Regardless of whether you're a neophyte or a seasoned public speaker, you can benefit from spending some time with this app.

Worst features

I would like the app even more if it contained more media — more illustrations, photos, and audio and video clips. Aside from that, though, I don't have anything to complain about.

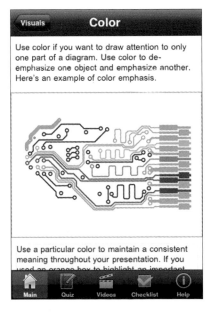

AltaMail
$9.99 US

AltaMail is a powerful alternative to the Mail app included with your iPhone. AltaMail offers an extensive list of unique features; the one I find most useful is the contact e-mail view, which lets me see all incoming and outgoing messages from or to any contact. Other powerful features of the app include multiple signatures with images, printing via your Mac or PC locally or remotely, zipping and unzipping file attachments, and attaching more than one image or file to a single message.

The more e-mail you send and receive on your iPhone, the more you'll appreciate AltaMail.

Documents to Go
$9.99 US

I think I tried every app that claims to be able to edit Microsoft Word and Excel files, and Documents to Go by DataViz is the only one that worked consistently and rendered documents accurately. It can create, open, and edit Word and Excel documents, including their latest file formats (.docx and .xlsx, respectively). It supports lots of character, paragraph, cell, and number formatting options; Wi-Fi sync; cut, copy, and paste; and multiple undo/redo options. The Word module supports predictive text, auto-correction, and auto-capitalization; the Excel module has 111 mathematical functions and supports multiple worksheets.

If you need to work with Microsoft Office documents, this is the app you want.

FTP On The Go
$6.99 US

FTP On The Go is a full-featured FTP client for your iPhone. It lets you browse, upload, and download files from any FTP server, using FTPS and data compression if the server supports them. Perhaps the most useful feature of FTP On The Go is its capability to download a text file, edit it using the app's built-in text editor, and re-upload the changed file. You can resize images before you upload them, and if you have an iPhone 3GS, you can even upload video. With bookmarks, password protection, and CHMOD permission editing, you can easily use FTP On The Go to manage a Web site with your iPhone, and that's way cool.

Print n Share
$6.99 US

If you ever have to print documents on your Mac or PC locally over your Wi-Fi network or remotely over 3G or EDGE, Print n Share is what you need. It includes a built-in Wi-Fi hard drive that lets you drag and drop files between your iPhone and your computer. It also lets you zip, unzip, and view .doc, .docx, .xls, .xlsx, .txt, .html, .PDF, and many other file types before you print them. With a Web browser that can print pages and offers flexible photo printing, Print n Share is the only way to go if you need to be able to print documents from your iPhone.

QuickVoice2Text Email (PRO Recorder)
$0.99 US

QuickVoice2Text Email (PRO Recorder) is one of my favorite and most-used apps. It lets you speak into your iPhone and then translates your spoken words to text before e-mailing both the recording and the text to anyone you choose. I use this app many times a day to send myself reminders of things I need to do or to create and send e-mail at times when it would be inconvenient or time-consuming to type them on my iPhone.

QuickVoice2Text Email works great, translates speech to text as accurately as anything I've ever used, and costs only 99¢. How can you not love that?

3 Education

Bobble Rep
$0.99 US

Boy, did this app cause a ruckus when it was first released — or wasn't released, as the case may be. At first, Apple rejected Bobble Rep for "ridiculing public figures." I guess that someone on the App Store approval team had never heard of a *caricature*. Fortunately, however, after the story broke and everybody and their brother in the blogosphere started talking about Bobble Rep, Apple reversed its decision and approved the app.

The decision to approve the app is a good thing. Bobble Rep isn't an engine of political commentary; it's a non-partisan, simple, and easy-to-use database for identifying and contacting your representative in the U.S. Congress, be he or she a Senator or Representative.

Tom Richmond created all the artwork for this app. If the images in Bobble Rep look familiar, you may know Tom from his work as a contributor to *MAD Magazine* or from the movie *Super Capers*. I just love the art in this app, and it seems to resonate with just about everyone who checks it out.

On the useful side, Bobble Rep — 111th Congress Edition (as it is officially called) offers contact information for every member of the 111th Congress (look for dedicated versions for future Congresses) from *A* (see the figure on the left) to *Z* (ditto the figure on the right). You can look up members by name, party-affiliation, state, class (the year their term ends), or address. You can even perform searches by using Current Location if you don't want to bother entering your full address.

TIP

Tilt your iPhone when viewing a member's page for the full bobblehead experience.

The easiest ways to pull up *your* members of Congress are to use the address or Current Location lookups. Although many of us (I'd like to think most of us) know who our Senators are, fewer people know their Representatives. Bobble Rep makes it easy to find out who's representing you in Washington.

After you pull up a member, you see the aforementioned caricature, detailed contact information — including a link to the member's official government-hosted Web site — a direct link to the official Web contact form, and all of the member's local offices, including phone numbers.

The sweet thing about the phone numbers is that they're iPhone links — just tap a number and your iPhone calls it for you. It's never been so easy to call your Congressional representatives. Contacting your members of Congress and letting them know your opinion on issues important to you is a valuable part of the political process, no matter which side of the aisle your Senator or Representative sits on.

Best features

Bobble Rep includes great art and information you need — it's a great combo!

Worst features

I'd like to be able to flick through the members of Congress in the information-pane mode, but I have a feeling the database is just too big for the iPhone to handle in that manner. I'd also like e-mail addresses to be listed in the contact information.

Civilization Revolution (Sid Meier)
$6.99 US

I can hear you now: "Hey mom, Dr. Mac says this iPhone game is educational!" Hey, it is educational, but it's also fun, which makes this app a win-win. The Civilization games have been around for a long time. Although the games are hardly a substitute for a history book, I think they present a practical lesson in the way economics work. Specifically, these games teach what is called Guns and Butter Economics, which is the balance governments must take between military and domestic spending.

See, you're learning something already! Anyway, all the Civilization games on the PC and Mac make players balance what they spend on the military (guns) and civilian needs (butter). Spend too much on one and the other suffers, which is likely to cost you the game. When you throw in the need to balance expansion with sustainable growth, there's even more to learn before you can master the game.

What I found most surprising about the iPhone version of Civilization is just how playable it is on a handheld device. Before I downloaded the app, I thought it would be too difficult to play on the iPhone; but the reality is that it's fun. The developers didn't try to shoehorn everything from the desktop game into the iPhone. Instead, they put a lot of thought into what makes an iPhone app work, as you can see in the figure.

The units are easy to control, movement is intuitive, cities are easy to manage, and even the combat makes sense. The planet size is big enough to be interesting, but it's not so big as to leave you feeling like you can't grasp everything. If you're brand new to the Civilization franchise, there's a built-in tutorial that explains everything you need to know without getting in the way.

When starting out, be sure to send a unit into the villages in order to find gold, free units (the best is a free Settler unit for what amounts to a free town in the beginning!), or technology. When your civilization is capable of deep-water ocean travel, look for the Lost City of Atlantis for several free advanced technologies.

The game includes several levels of difficulty, and you can choose which leaders or culture you want to play. The game also offers a scenario mode with predefined goals that change up the game play quite a bit. After you've mastered the game, try Beta-Centauri mode, where you start off on a fresh planet, but you already know all the technologies!

I'm telling you, this game really surprised me in how much fun it is. The only downside is that I found the game crashed frequently near the end of long play. As of this writing, the game doesn't have an auto-save feature, so I found myself manually saving frequently to keep from having to replay lost game-years when the game crashed.

I hope that by the time you read this book, auto-saves will have been added in an update. But even if the game still lacks auto-save, get this app anyway. You'll love it, and you may actually learn a thing or two!

There's a free Lite version for those who want to try before they buy. It's feature-limited and doesn't have a save-game feature, so the Lite version isn't a substitute for the real thing. But it does show you what the game play is like.

Best features

Fun, intuitive game play brings the best aspects of the Civilization franchise to your iPhone in a way that makes sense. You'll wonder where the time goes when you're playing the game.

Worst features

The lack of an auto-save feature can result in the loss of turns played at the end of very long games.

Dictionary!
Simons. Tir Top Pieter.

Dictionary!
Free

Maybe it's because I write for a living, but I've always felt a good dictionary is priceless; and the ability to carry one in my pocket may be one of the best aspects of having an iPhone!

Several dictionary apps are available for the iPhone, but I picked Dictionary! because it's free (it's ad supported) and easy to use. It includes more than 200,000 words and phrases, and the definitions are purposefully short and simple.

The interface is straightforward. To look up a word or phrase, you type it in a field, and the results appear in real-time.

When you find the word you want, tap it, and the definition is displayed at the bottom of the screen, as shown in the figure on the left. See the blue line (with a little ∧ in the middle of it) that separates the definition from the search results? As you drag the line toward the top of the screen, it opens the definitions pane to full screen so that you can more easily read the results (see the figure on the right below). This is especially handy for words that have several definitions.

The 200,000 definitions I mentioned earlier are included in the app itself, so Dictionary! works whether or not you are online or have a cell connection with your iPhone. The English language has more than 800,000 words, however, and when you are online, Dictionary! can perform lookups on Wiktionary.com for definitions that aren't in the app. To access the online lookup, open the definition pane and click the Open Wiktionary in Safari button in the lower-right corner of the window.

Another cool feature is the capability to copy a definition for use in another iPhone app, such as Mail or a Twitter app. Touch and hold on a definition, and the iPhone OS 3.0 copy box appears around the definition. Touch the Copy button that appears, and the definition is saved to your clipboard for you to use elsewhere.

All in all, Dictionary! is a great example of a dictionary for your iPhone.

When you first run the app, it spends a few minutes building an index of itself. This is a file-size–saving feature the developers used to keep the app small enough to download over a 3G network. After Dictionary! runs this indexing process, you won't have to do it again.

Best features

Short and useful definitions make for fast lookups and quick understanding. The ability to look up additional definitions on Wiktionary.com is handy for those rare times when you need to look up a word that's not included in the internal definitions.

Worst features

The ads take up screen real estate, but that's a small price to pay for such a useful, free app.

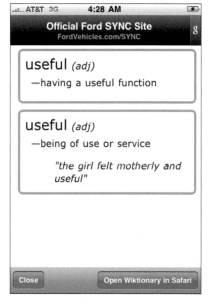

Musée du Louvre
Free

Musée du Louvre offers a detailed look at the museum that most of us call "The Louvre" or "Le Louvre." One of the world's most famous museums, Le Louvre houses the *Mona Lisa*, *Venus de Milo*, *Diana Leaving Her Bath*, and about a gillion other pieces of art, from small to great.

The iPhone app, which was published by the museum itself, offers what is effectively a brief, but detailed, tour of the museum. The tour includes images, video, information about the palace (it was built in the 12th Century as a fortress, and eventually housed French royalty, including some of the Napolean family), and handy visitor information about the museum.

I gravitate to the artwork section, which is presented in an iPhone Cover Flow format. Starting with the *Mona Lisa* front and center, you can flip through a score or so of the major artworks on display at the museum. Tap an individual painting, sculpture, or other piece of art, and a larger image of the work opens. Tap the larger image, and you get a new pane with buttons for About the Work (as shown in the figure), See More Detail, Technical Information, and Location.

You can use the buttons to get a history of the work, including who created it, what it is about, and what kinds of material were used to create it. The See More Detail button offers close-up images of the art, which you can zoom in on by using the iPhone's pinch gestures. The Location button reveals a map that shows where the artwork is displayed in the museum. All these features are really cool.

But wait, there's more! Musée du Louvre includes several high-definition videos of different pieces of art and parts of the museum. In a great use of Apple technology, each video is narrated in French, English, German, and Japanese. Note that the default language is French, but you can change it by tapping the information icon on the playback controls — this feature isn't readily apparent, so many people think the videos are offered only in French. The videos are all very cool, and my only complaint is that there aren't more of them.

The Palace section of the app offers a detailed look at the major sections of the building that houses the museum. Tap a selection in Cover Flow mode, and you get a picture with options for a short history, detailed pictures you can flip through, a video (if one is available — you're linked to the same videos mentioned earlier), and a map of the section in the museum.

If you find something you particularly like or want to come back to, you can bookmark entries by tapping the star on the entry's main page. You can access bookmarks from the main window of the app.

If you're lucky enough to be going to Le Louvre in person, the app offers directions, hours of operation, admission fees, information about the different services and amenities offered, as well as contact information. Being able to access this information makes this app invaluable to anyone who's going to see the real deal.

The text in the app is searchable, which makes it easy to find what you're looking for.

If you're interested in art or French history and architecture (including all the gilded gaudiness of royal excess in the 18th and 19th centuries), Musée de Louvre is a great way to see some of what's in this world-famous museum.

Best features

The wealth of information contained in the app is wonderful, and the developers made it easy to access. Better yet, it's free.

Worst features

The app has so much content in it, flipping through the information can sometimes cause the app to stutter. Also, because of all the content, the app is a big download (62MB).

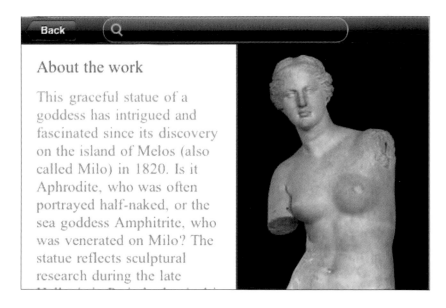

Star Walk
$4.99 US

Hey, is that the universe in your pocket, or are you just happy to see me? OK, OK, I kid, but having Star Walk on my iPhone really does make me feel like I have the universe at my fingertips!

Star Walk is part digital telescope, part sky-map, and part star database. You can look up stars and constellations, and you can even get information on the auroras and other atmospheric phenomenon. The app also includes information on the moon phases and enables you to look at the sky as you are seeing it tonight or as it will look one year from now.

When you launch Star Walk, you see a segment of the night sky as it appears based on your Location Services info. You can drag the map around to see different parts of the sky, and you can double tap to zoom in closer to more easily see individual stars.

For instance, I found Rigel (because it was featured in a *Star Trek* episode — I know, I'm a geek!), and double tapped it until I could see it and only a handful of other stars. By clicking the *i* button in the top left, I learned some geeky info such as Rigel is in the Orion constellation and it has a visual magnitude of 0.1.

The stars are displayed with their actual colors, and major features of the night sky are labeled for you. As you move the map around, abstract representations of the constellations and other features appear in real-time.

Information about the planets includes their order in the solar system, mass, radius, and surface temperature.

One of the coolest features of this app is limited to the iPhone 3GS because that version of the iPhone has a compass and the built-in GPS system. When you tilt your iPhone 3GS, the Star Spotter feature shows you a representation of the part of the sky your iPhone is pointed at! Move your iPhone, and the starfield moves with you! That's just too cool!

Other features include the Pic of the Day, which is really the last several astronomy Pics of the Day. Choose a picture from the list, and if you are connected to the Internet via cell network or Wi-Fi the picture displays. Tap the *i* button, and you get detailed information about the image.

If you want to look up stars, planets, or constellations by name, you can do that, too. Just tap the magnifying glass when you're on the main screen, and a searchable list appears with tabs for different categories at the bottom. After you find the celestial object you want, tap it, and the star map re-appears, centered on the object you selected.

Some celestial bodies have Wikipedia entries. When you're in the *i* information, tap the *w* button where one is available and the celestial body's Wikipedia entry opens in Safari.

You can spin the app about 180 degrees and look at a detailed globe of the planet Earth. The globe pinpoints your location and offers real-time information on the day and night parts of the planet. Tap the magnifying glass, and you can look up a specific city, complete with latitude and longitude, and then you can look at the sky from that city's location. It's just crazy what you can do with this app!

Lastly, there's a built-in help function that gives you detailed information about how to use all the features this great app offers.

Best features

Star Spotter is way, way too much fun, and I love being able to get information about the stars I can see right above me.

Worst features

Due to the amount of information the app has to load, it takes several seconds to launch, but that's not really much of a complaint.

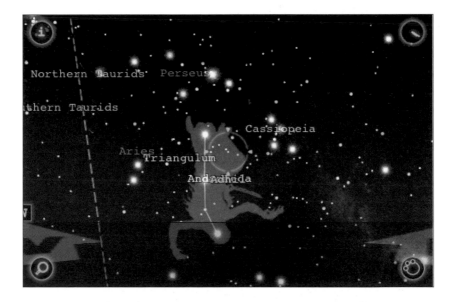

French 101
$7.99 US

French 101 is part of a series of foreign language-learning apps for the iPhone called 24/7 Tutor. This series of apps includes French, German, Italian, and Spanish, and each language has four different levels: Free, 101, 102, and 103.

I looked at French 101 and Free French Tutor and found them to be solid, no-frills apps for learning French words (French 103 offers phrases). French 101 includes several categories of words or phrases and has four different modes for quizzing you on those words — repetition is part of the learning process. You get a quiz grade when you complete each mode so you can track your learning.

The Free versions of the app include only 25 words and are really little more than a sampler that shows you the approach the developers use.

HP 12C Financial Calculator
$14.99 US

This app is part super-useful for people in finance (where the HP 12C is still in use) and part blast-from-your-past for those of us old enough to remember when a handheld calculator cost as much, if not more, than an iPhone!

The HP 12C is a programmable calculator that enables you to enter long and complex formulas for values that are common in the financial industry (from loan payments to cash blow, to bond values, and much, much more).

The app version of this venerable calculator includes everything the original does and less — you can tilt your iPhone to get a simplified RPN calculator.

Matches
Free

If you're familiar with the card game Concentration, you know Matches. The great thing about the app, though, is that you don't have to gather up and deal the cards each time! Matches is a simple matching game that has bright, simple illustrations. Kids are the target audience.

Each game board has two of each letter, number, animal, or transportation-themed image, and the point of the game is to pair matching squares. The hitch, of course, is that if you choose two squares that don't match, they turn back over — you have to remember where they are for future matching. The faster you make matches, the higher your score, and playing the game may improve your memory.

 # Math Flash Cards
$0.99 US

As the name suggests, Math Flash Cards is a flash card app for simple math (addition, subtraction, multiplication, and division). It includes a multiple-choice mode, as well as numeric keypad entry for math fun that's a little more challenging.

The app keeps track of how long it takes you to finish each level, which is a great benchmarking carrot for kids to try to beat. You can also set up new decks of cards, each with its own options.

The interface is clean and simple, and Math Flash Cards is useful for young children who are learning math.

 TIP To turn on the numeric keypad mode, click the arrow next to your deck and turn off Multiple Choice.

 # Wheels on the Bus
$0.99 US

Wheels on the Bus is an interactive book based on the song of the same name. This app plays the song, and each stanza gets its own interactive page with elements you can poke or drag.

For instance, "The doors on the bus go open and shut" features doors you can slide open and close, with a bird you can see after the door is open. Very young kids will love Wheels on the Bus.

The drawings are bright and colorful, and the app features several languages (including gibberish), instruments, and the capability for you (or your kid) to record the song yourself!

4 Entertainment

Acrobots
$0.99 US

The application description in the iTunes App Store for Acrobots says it's a "mesmerizing, physics-based toy," and I'll be darned if I can think of a more accurate description.

The so-called acrobots (or "bots" for short) are multicolored, gelatinous, acrobatic creatures with circle bodies and three slender arms that have suction cups at the ends (see the image on the left). The bots tumble, disconnect, reconnect, push off one another and the edges of the screen, and float around in a smooth, colorful ballet.

By tilting or shaking your iPhone, you can make the bots move on their own based on the settings you specify (as shown in the figure on the right). You can also tap any bot to flick it in any direction; the faster you flick, the faster the bot moves.

The five icons shown (from left to right) at the top of the screen in the images on the next page perform these tasks:

- ✔ **Plus sign:** Adds a bot.

- ✔ **Minus sign:** Removes a bot.

- ✔ **Light bulb:** Turns silhouette mode on and off. In silhouette mode, the bots turn a dark shade of blue and the background changes from black to light blue.

- ✔ **Target:** Opens the settings screen.

- ✔ **Question mark:** Displays the version number.

The settings screen, shown on the right, lets you control the physics that govern the bots' movement. You have complete control over the bots' size, balance, suction cup stickiness, and movement speed, as well as the effects of gravity and air drag.

At the bottom of the screen are eight presets that control all six parameters at once. The setting I used in the figure on the right below is called Beasts; others include Teeter, Tumble, Spazz.

If you're having trouble imagining what bots look like in motion, check out the Web-based Flash simulation of Acrobots at `www.vectorpark.com/acrobots`. There you can add and remove bots, flick them, and adjust their speed. But because you can't tilt or shake your computer, nor can you control individual physics attributes of the bots, the simulation isn't nearly as cool as the iPhone version. Despite these shortcomings, it's still a good demo of what bot movements look like. If you need to be convinced that this app is cool, give the demo a try.

Best features

Acrobots is mesmerizing, fascinating, and, at least in my humble opinion, soothing. I can waste an inordinate amount of time flinging them around, shaking my iPhone to scramble them, and observing the effects different settings have on the way the bots move. The app is also great for showing people something "cool" on your iPhone.

Worst features

I think the effect of Acrobots would be even more stunning if there were sounds associated with suction cups attaching to and detaching from other suction cups, but the app doesn't include audio. That said, you can play music with your iPod while you play with Acrobots, which doesn't have the same effect as app-specific audio would, but it's still interesting.

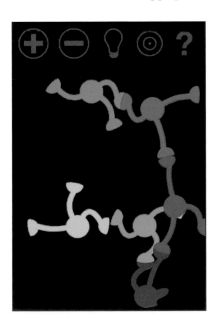
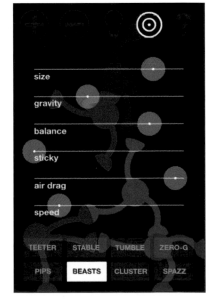

Backgrounds
Free

Backgrounds is an app that gives you access to more than 9,000 mostly high-quality images you can use as wallpaper on your iPhone. For those of you who aren't interested in customizing your wallpaper or iPhone Contacts photos, you might want to skip this app. However, if you're still seeing the blue globe in the background because you didn't realize you could put something else in its place, read on.

The iPhone has always given you the capability to choose a custom wallpaper image. If you open the Settings app, tap Wallpaper, and then tap Wallpaper again, you can see that your iPhone includes 18 wallpaper images in addition to the aforementioned blue globe. Alternatively, you can tap Camera Roll or Photo Library instead of tapping Wallpaper the second time and use any photo in your library as wallpaper.

I love iPhone wallpaper and change mine often to fit my mood. Today I have a picture of an Aston-Martin DB9 that I've been lusting for; last week I had a snow leopard; the week before that I had the fabulous nature shot shown on the left. The one thing all three wallpaper images have in common is that I got them free with the Backgrounds app.

You can search by keyword or browse the most popular and most recently added images by tapping the appropriate button at the top of the screen, as shown in the figure on the right. You can also browse in more than 30 categories, including Funny, Quotes, Love, Animals, Cars, Cute, For Guys, Artsy, Nature, Patterns, and Buildings.

As you browse, the images are displayed four at a time, as shown on the right. Tap the left- or right-arrow buttons at the bottom of the screen to see the next or previous group of four images. When you find an image that looks interesting, tap it to check out a full-size preview, as shown in the image on the left. When you find an image you like, tap the Save button and the image is saved to your iPhone's Camera Roll. To use the image as your wallpaper, launch the Settings app, tap Wallpaper, tap Camera Roll, and tap the image. Whenever you unlock your phone or talk to someone you don't have a picture of, you see the wallpaper image rather than the blue globe or whatever other picture you previously had selected.

When you're browsing the images, if you tap the little asterisk button between the left and right arrows, you see a unique category of images called Frames. A frame is an image with a hole in it. You can insert a photo of yourself or anyone else into the hole in the image. Choose the photo you want to use and Backgrounds lets you move, scale, and rotate the picture to fit it in the frame. Presto! You now have a unique wallpaper image that integrates the person of your choosing. It's a pretty cool idea and is nicely implemented here.

With more than 9,000 background images and more added daily, the Background app ensures that you'll never run out of fresh images to use as wallpaper on your iPhone.

Best features

How can you not love a free app that provides thousands of free wallpaper images, plus thoughtful touches such as Frames?

Worst features

The app and wallpaper images are free, but the app isn't free of intrusive ads, as shown at the bottom of both images. There are also a number of somewhat lame pictures in the app, but it's not difficult to ignore them.

Brushes
$4.99 US

Brushes is a drawing and painting app designed exclusively for the iPhone. With a simple, elegant user interface, Brushes offers a powerful toolset for drawing and painting — as you can see in the four sample images that come with the app, shown in the figure on the left, reduced to one-quarter size.

Thoughtful touches abound in Brushes. Tap once anywhere on the screen to show or hide the toolbar. Zoom in as much as 1,600% or out to 70% with the iPhone pinch and unpinch gestures. Pick a color with a single press of your fingertip.

The app is called Brushes, so the obvious place to start exploring is with the brush styles. The app has three types — smooth, fine bristle, and rough bristle — which are available in any size from 1 to 64 pixels and offer complete control over the opacity of your strokes.

There's a terrific color picker (shown in the figure on the right). To change the hue and saturation of the color you want to use for painting, drag the knob (a little white circle) around on the color wheel. Below the color wheel are two sliders. The top slider determines the brightness of the selected color and the bottom slider determines the color's opacity.

Many desktop graphics programs have an eyedropper tool to "pick up" any color in your image and paint with it. There's an eyedropper in the Brushes toolbar, too, but I almost always use the shortcut of pressing my finger in one spot for half a second, which causes the eyedropper tool to pop up directly under my fingertip.

Another cool feature of Brushes is its support for up to four layers. I've seen layers in many desktop graphics programs, but Brushes is the first iPhone app I've seen with 'em. Each layer can be painted independently without affecting the layers above or below. You drag and drop to change the stacking order of the layers, which I find both elegant and intuitive. You have full control over layer opacity, so you can use a semitransparent layer to tint all or part of the layer(s) below. And you can merge any of the layers with any other(s) at anytime.

Don't worry if you make a mistake — Brushes has at least ten levels of undo and redo, so you can undo or redo your last ten (or more) actions.

When you're finished with your masterpiece, you can save it in the Brushes gallery so you can easily work on it some more or show it to your friends with the Brushes built-in slideshow. You can export finished pictures to your iPhone's Camera Roll or use the Brushes built-in Web server to view or download your creations over Wi-Fi with any Web browser on any computer.

If you're a Mac OS X user, there's a cool free Brushes Viewer that lets you view or export your paintings on your Mac. Another interesting feature is that the Brushes Viewer can display a stroke-by-stroke animated replay of the making of your painting, which you can export as a QuickTime movie. Plus, the Brushes Viewer can export paintings at up to six times their iPhone resolution (1,920 x 2,880 pixels).

The best way to experience Brushes is to check out some of the work that's been done with it. Take a look at the cover of the June 1, 2009 issue of *The New Yorker* (http://tinyurl.com/brushes-newyorker), which shows art created with Brushes by artist Jorge Colombo. Then watch this video clip from ABC News (http://tinyurl.com/brushes-abc) and check out what other Brushes users have created in this Flickr group (http://flickr.com/groups/brushes). Finally, take a gander at what pop artist David Hockney has done with Brushes (http://www.nybooks.com/features/slideshows/hockney).

Best features
The best feature of Brushes is its simple but powerful user interface. If you're artistically inclined, there's no limit to the things you can create with Brushes.

Worst features
The way-cool Brushes Viewer isn't available for Windows.

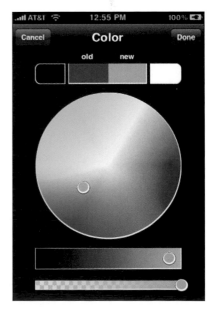

EyeTV
$4.99* US

The EyeTV app provides three awesome TV-related features. With it I can

- ✔ Use my iPhone to watch TV shows and movies I've recorded using EyeTV on my Mac without having to sync or transfer them to my iPhone

- ✔ Remotely start recording live TV or schedule a future recording on my Mac at home

- ✔ Watch live TV on my iPhone wherever I have Wi-Fi

Before you get too excited about EyeTV, know that there are a couple of provisos. See the asterisk next to the $4.99 price? It's there because to use this app you must have the EyeTV software and hardware running on your Mac at home. The EyeTV hardware and software packages, which let you watch and record television programming on your Mac screen, cost at least $149.95.

Having had the EyeTV hardware and software on my Mac for many years — long before the iPhone was invented — I've felt it was worth every penny. Today I think that the EyeTV hardware and software on my Mac plus the EyeTV iPhone app may be the greatest combination since peanut butter and jelly. It's an awesome combo even at $154.94 ($149.95 + $4.99).

I love watching video on my iPhone, especially when I'm stuck in a hotel room far from home. Before the EyeTV app, I had to stock my iPhone with any movies or TV shows I might want to watch in my hotel. Now I don't have to do that. Instead, I just fire up the EyeTV app on my iPhone and choose from the hundreds of movies and TV shows I've recorded with EyeTV on my Mac, including dozens of episodes of *The Family Guy*, as shown in the figure on the left. I also have access to dozens of theatrical movies I've recorded.

Speaking of recording, the EyeTV app lets me start a recording at home or schedule one for the future. It includes a built-in program guide that shows me what's on for the next 10 days. If there's something I want to record, I just tap the Record button and the EyeTV system on my Mac records it. Shortly after the show ends, I can watch it on my iPhone.

Another cool feature of the EyeTV app is that I can watch live TV anywhere there's Wi-Fi. When I'm sitting at Starbucks enjoying a latte, I can watch the news live on any of my local TV channels or watch CNN, MTV, VH1, or any of the other 70+ channels available with EyeTV.

All these features add up to a fabulous TV experience on my iPhone.

Best features

The best feature is using the EyeTV app on my iPhone to schedule and record TV shows on my Mac and watch them at my convenience on my iPhone. Though watching live TV on my iPhone is pretty darn cool, too.

Worst features

First, the app requires you to also have an EyeTV hardware and software system ($149.95+). Second, EyeTV systems are Mac-only. And third, the app doesn't work over 3G or EDGE, only over Wi-Fi.

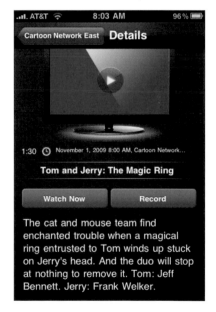

Now Playing
Free

A number of apps provide information about the movies playing in your local theatres. I've tried lots of them, and the app I keep coming back to is Now Playing. It has everything you need to help you decide on a movie, theatre, and show time.

You can browse the movies playing in your area by title, release date, or rating, as shown in the figure on the left. I've selected ratings and reviews from Rotten Tomatoes (www.rottentomatoes.com), but you can choose to receive your ratings and reviews from Metacritic or Google. If you tap the arrow to the right of a ranked listing, you can read a description of the movie (see figure on the right).

If you tap the Theatres button at the bottom of the screen, you can see movie theatres (instead of movie titles) sorted by your choice of the theatre name or distance from your current location. This feature is great when you're out to dinner or visiting a friend across town and you want to find out what movies are playing at theatres nearby.

Maps and driving directions are available for all theatres, or you can see an overview map that shows all nearby theatres at once.

When you find a movie you're interested in, with a single tap you can

- ✔ Watch its trailer
- ✔ Read reviews of it from a variety of print and online sources
- ✔ Have the theatres and show-time listings e-mailed to you
- ✔ View in Safari the Amazon, IMDb, Metacritic, Rotten Tomatoes, or Wikipedia Web page for the movie

You can even buy your tickets for many (but not all) theatres with a couple more taps.

But that's not all. Now Playing works with any network connection (Wi-Fi, EDGE, or 3G). After you've opened the app and downloaded the latest movie data, you can view the information again even when you don't have a network connection of any type.

If you're a Netflix user, you have the capability to add movies to your Netflix queue right from the Now Playing app.

You can also browse through future movie releases sorted alphabetically by title or chronologically by release date.

Finally, you can browse new DVD releases alphabetically by title or chronologically by release date.

I use this app almost every time I'm thinking of going to a movie. I love being able to see all the movies playing nearby, ranked by their Rotten Tomatoes rating. It's great to be able to watch movie trailers wherever I happen to be when the movie-going mood strikes me. Luckily, most of the theatres near my house offer online ticketing, so I can usually snag tickets in advance and avoid waiting in line or being disappointed when the movie I want to see sells out before I get there.

The app is free and it's great. If you like movies, you'll love Now Playing.

Best features

All the features are great. Having movie listings with show times for all nearby theatres is handy, as well as being able to watch trailers and see movie reviews and ratings on your iPhone. Even though you can't always buy tickets to a particular movie at a specific theatre, when you can buy tickets using your iPhone, it's especially convenient.

Worst features

I honestly can't think of a single bad feature. There aren't even any ads to gripe about — unless you consider movie trailers to be ads. And even if you do consider trailers to be ads (because they are), they're one of the very few types of ads I actually like to watch.

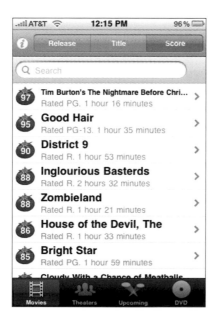

Koi Pond
$0.99 US

Picture a beautiful crystal-clear pond with colorful koi fish swimming in the shallow water as you listen to the soft sounds of nature in the background. Next, imagine sticking a finger in the water and watching the water ripple as the koi dart away.

Now picture what this scenario might be like on your iPhone, and you have Koi Pond. With myriad options, the app looks and sounds great, and it is surprisingly calming. You can set its sleep timer and allow yourself to drift off while listening to the soothing sounds of water, frogs, birds, insects, and rain.

Gorgeous, relaxing, and beautiful — what more could you ask from a 99¢ app?

Lightsaber Unleashed
Free

If you're a *Star Wars* fan or just someone who thinks lightsabers are the coolest weapon since the mace, you'll love the Lightsaber Unleashed app.

You'll thrill to the sounds of an actual Lightsaber as you swing your iPhone to and fro. The app even makes the right sounds when you turn your lightsaber on or off.

There's optional *Star Wars*-like music and your choice of Force Unleashed characters (Darth Vader, Shaak Ti, Rahm Kota, and so on). In addition, you can choose the color and hilt style of your lightsaber.

It's a silly app, but if you're a *Star Wars* fan, it's a must-have.

Rising Card
$2.99 US

Ask a friend to name any playing card. Tap the Rising Card icon and a deck of playing cards appears. Sprinkle some magic whiffle dust on it or say some magic words and then ask your friend to give the iPhone a gentle shake. Your friend will be amazed when his card floats out of the deck.

The illusion is easy to perform; it works every time; and the secret (which, of course, I won't reveal) is diabolical.

Many people suspect the app works with voice recognition, but it doesn't. A person can write down the card's name instead of saying it aloud, and the illusion still works perfectly.

This is truly one of my very favorite apps.

TMZ
Free

The TMZ app has a single purpose: to deliver up-to-the-minute entertainment news, photos, and videos directly to your iPhone.

Its simple interface provides easy access to breaking entertainment news that's updated 24/7, and it includes dedicated video and photo galleries and TMZ TV.

This app takes celebrity gossip to a new high (or low). Rest assured that if a scandal breaks out anywhere in the world, you'll hear about it first with the TMZ app.

Whether you're a fan of TMZ.com, a celebrity gossip lover, a Hollywood glitz gourmet, or just someone who loves seeing dirt dished, you'll love the TMZ app.

2000+ Sounds
$0.99 US

Yep, it's just what its name implies — an app with more than 2,000 sound effects. These are not just any sound effects, though; they're high-quality, professionally recorded sounds.

The sounds are nicely organized in descriptive categories. You can also search for sounds by name. If you're not in the mood for anything particular, there's a random sounds button.

All sounds can be looped to repeat indefinitely, and you can create a list of your favorite sounds.

My favorite feature is the timer, which allows me to pick a sound and delay its start for as long as 120 seconds. Think of all the fun you'll have with this feature . . . or not.

2000+ Sounds is silly and sophomoric, but it's still kind of fun.

5 Finance

Bank of Mom
$1.99 US

The Bank of Mom app has a great name and a great purpose, and I hope that lots of moms (and dads) take this app to heart. What this app does is allow parents to keep track of their kids' bank accounts, or rather their kids' virtual bank accounts. The app documents everything that comes into and goes out of those accounts, including deposits and withdrawals, why they were made, and interest accrued by an account. You can also get an e-mail of the transaction history.

The point of the app, according to the developers, is to help parents teach kids what money is, where it comes from, where it goes, what it's worth, and what it really means to earn interest on an account. Think about that for a second: How many of you know kids (or, for that matter, adults) who have no inkling of how to budget, where their money comes from and goes to, and exactly how a credit card works?

I've heard parents, and even news stories, talk about this very thing. The point of Bank of Mom is to introduce these topics to kids at an early age so that they have time to learn about budgeting before being tossed out into the world with a mailbox full of credit card applications. I think educating kids about money is a great idea, and I wish my mom had had a tool like this when I was a kid.

I really should mention that the Bank of Mom app enables parents to do the same sort of tracking with time. In other words, you can set up an account for watching TV or being on the Internet, with "deposits" for time earned (by doing chores and mowing the lawn, for example) and withdrawals for using that time.

Let's look at how the app works. You set up one or more accounts in the main window. In the figure on the left (although the names are truncated in the screen shot), I have these accounts set up:

Samantha's Savings Account, Timmy, and Timmy's TV Time. The balance for each account is shown in the figure — $59.62 for Samantha, $449.88 for Timmy, and 15 minutes for Timmy's TV Time.

When I tap Timmy, I see the most recent three transactions, as you can see in the figure on the right. The top entry is a deposit for $30 from a loving aunt; the middle entry is the $20 he spent at the movies; and the bottom entry is the starting balance for the account. The current balance is in the reddish bar above the entries. The entries are easy to make, and there's an optional description field you can use for a comment or other information. The whole app is easy to read and understand.

Try entering an interest payment when your child is watching — seeing $8.92 in interest added to the account could provide a meaningful lesson.

Best features

The best feature of Bank of Mom is really the concept itself, which is a simple way to track money (or time) in a way that makes it easier for kids to learn the value of money.

Worst features

In the iTunes reviews, a lot of people complain about the lack of instructions (which are actually right there in iTunes), but I personally found the app to be intuitive.

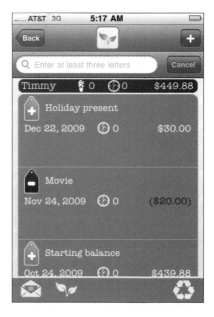

Bloomberg

Free

If you want to watch your stocks but don't have an E*Trade or other online brokerage account, you may want to consider Bloomberg, the self-titled app from the Bloomberg wire service. This app offers stock quotes, market information, and financial news.

Let me start with that last item: news. I'm one of those old-school guys who thinks that news is important, and Bloomberg really seems to know how to handle the news. The company offers some of the best financial news on the planet, and it has been expanding into other areas beyond the scope of this iPhone app.

Bloomberg offers the news in a number of different ways. Of course, you can get company-specific news when you view a stock, but in the News tab, you can get a list of news headlines and filter it in more than a score of ways. For instance, when you first fire up the app, you only see Worldwide and Exclusive categories. However, you can also list news according to most read, bonds, commodities, currencies, the economy, emerging markets, energy, funds, health care, insurance, municipal bonds, politics, opinions, and more. You can filter by 13 different countries. You can even get audio news right in the app, which is a killer feature, in my opinion.

There's also a tab for Markets, which is shown in the figure on the left. The app includes the six exchanges and indices listed in the screenshot, as well as another 40 or so markets and indices from around the world. Note the last column, which is percent changed (% Chg). See the little orange triangle above the column? That triangle lets you toggle through options to see the change in terms of points and the time at which the numbers in the Last column were registered. If you tap an individual listing, say DOW JONES, the app opens up to a page that offers you just about everything you might want to know about that market's performance for the day, as well as a short paragraph explaining what it is you're looking at, which is very handy for those who don't know. I am surprised, though, that the page doesn't default to news (like it does for stocks), nor allow you to tap the news items for an explanation.

Speaking of stocks, with the Bloomberg app you can put together a list of stocks you want to watch. In the figure on the bottom right, I put in Apple, Microsoft, AT&T, and BlackBerry maker Research in Motion (I know, I know, but on the day I took these screenshots, that was the first company I could find that closed up, and I wanted you to see the differences in the way the data is shown). When you choose the stocks, you can enter how many shares you own and the price at which you bought them. To see the value of your holdings, tap the orange triangles at the top of the columns for some additional options.

Even with all its great features, the Bloomberg app is not the best app for monitoring the value of your portfolio. It is, however, a great way to monitor your portfolio's day-to-day performance and to get general interest financial news and news relating to your stocks.

Best features

The color scheme is easy to read and easy on the eye, and the features are all easy to use. If you want fast financial news, this app is for you.

Worst features

When searching for companies to watch in your stock list, the app doesn't give you an error when it can't find any matches, which is totally unintuitive. I'd like it if some of the features were easier to find, too.

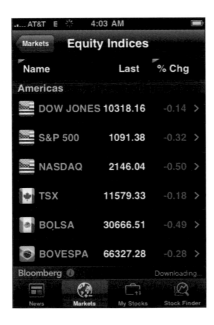

CompareMe – Shopping Utility
$1.99 US

I'm writing this book in the midst of the worst economic downturn since the Great Depression, and I haven't seen people be so tight with their money since the recession of the 1970s. In an economic environment like this, it certainly makes sense to shop smartly and do as much comparison pricing as possible.

These days, a lot of supermarkets make comparison shopping easier than it used to be by offering a cost breakdown (by the ounce or unit count) of most products. Not all stores offer that service, though, and sometimes you aren't readily presented with the information you need to make good choices.

For instance, I like to buy whole coffee beans and grind them at home, and recently I've been enjoying brewing espresso with Italian Roast beans from Peet's Coffee and Tea. I can buy the beans directly from the coffee shop for roughly $12.99 per pound; but then I noticed that a bag of the same beans at the grocery store is only $9.99!

After doing some research, however, I discovered that the grocery store bags are 12 ounces, not a pound (16 ounces). But I still didn't know which was less expensive per ounce. And that, my friends, is a perfect example of when you need CompareMe!

As you can see in the figure on the left, by buying my coffee beans directly from a Peet's shop, I can save two percent.

Oh sure, I could compare the prices by hand, but CompareMe makes these kinds of comparisons so easy, I've found myself using the app more and more often, which is making me a better shopper. In this case, I try to buy my beans directly from Peet's whenever I can. Two percent here and two percent there definitely adds up over the long haul!

Do you like tuna? I do! But, boy, the pricing on canned tuna can fluctuate wildly. And don't be deceived by those larger cans. You'd think they would be cheaper by the ounce than the smaller cans, but CompareMe has shown that's never the case unless the large cans are on sale. The same is often true about toothpaste, which surprised the heck out of me. Buying something in larger quantities is usually cheaper, but not always. So be sure to do your comparisons with CompareMe.

CompareMe offers a detailed breakdown for each comparison it does. In the figure on the bottom right, you can see a side-by-side comparison of the A versus B pricing in their respective sizes, along with a breakdown of the price in its smallest form, which in this case is the ounce.

CompareMe has built-in values for grams, milligrams, kilograms, metric tonnes, ounces, pounds, short hundredweight, short tons, quarters, long hundredweights, long tons, and pfunds. Yeah, yeah — I didn't know what those weird measurements were, either, but a quick Google search showed me they are mostly shipping and customs terms.

Best features

CompareMe is easy to use, and it provides quick comparisons when I'm doing my shopping.

Worst features

I'd like to be able to compare more than two things at a time.

E*Trade Mobile Pro
Free*

In the beginning, trading of stocks was done between two people (men, usually, at that time) who would meet and buy or sell shares in a company. Then came the Age of the Broker, a highly paid person whose biggest asset was access to a person with a trading seat on one of the stock exchanges. At some point after the Internet became mainstream, companies such as E*Trade took the place of the broker, offering the same sort of access at a much lower price because all the work was being done through computers instead of face-to-face or on the phone.

Today, if you have a computer with access to the Internet, you can effectively conduct your own stock transactions almost instantaneously. (Okay, a bunch of stuff is still being handled behind the scenes, but for all intents and purposes the transactions are instantaneous.)

Maybe instead of "today" I should have said "before the iPhone," because with apps like E*Trade Mobile Pro, you can now use your iPhone to access just about every single thing that used to require a computer. You can buy and sell stocks and options, transfer money between your E*Trade accounts, set up or manage watch lists, monitor your orders, manage and receive alerts, monitor your portfolio, get stock quotes, and get news — all from within this well-designed and elegant iPhone app.

I'm telling you, it's good to be alive today because an app like this was science fiction not so long ago.

Take a look at the figure on the left. What you see is the main Dashboard page, which offers quick access to all three major U.S. stock indexes (DOW, NASDAQ, and S&P 500), with options for viewing it for one day, one week, one month, three months, six months, one year, or two years. At the top is a side-scrolling panel for 15 different features, including your portfolio, the buying and selling screen, news, money transfers, and so on. The scrolling panel is smooth and works very well. At the bottom is a link to recent general interest financial news articles.

The figure on the right is an individual stock page, in this case for Apple Inc. (I know, I picked a rare losing day to take these screenshots.) On a stock page you get the most important information for monitoring the daily movement of a stock, including the last trade price (in this case, the closing price), which is color-coded for quick recognition (red for down, green for up, unshaded for no change). You also get current trading volume, the day's trading range, 52-week high and low, and the current market capitalization (the value) of the company.

Below the summary are two convenient buttons: use the Set Alert button to notify you when a stock hits a designated price, and use the Place Trade button to go to the buy and sell window for this particular stock. Below these buttons is the news list of recent articles for this particular company.

As the asterisk next to *Free* above indicates, "Free" isn't totally accurate because most of these features also require an E*Trade account. Without an account, you can't buy or sell stocks, maintain a portfolio of stocks, or get alerts. What you can do without an account, however, is get stock quotes, read company news articles, and see the stock indexes.

If you do have an account, there's a setting for whether your login information should be saved (be careful with that one!).

Best features

This app is like having a full-service stockbroker in your pocket! E*Trade Mobile Pro is easy to use and very, very well designed.

Worst features

I can't think of anything I don't like about this app, and that's saying something.

Economy
$0.99 US

Okay, I'm going to err on the esoteric side of things with this app, called Economy. Unlike most of the other apps in the Financial section of this book, Economy doesn't really help you do anything or keep track of anything. Instead, it gives you easy access to more than 40 American and Canadian economic reports — the kind of reports that you've probably heard mentioned in the news dozens of times but have never actually seen.

Why are these reports important? Some of us like to follow the kinds of things covered in them, either out of personal interest or for professional reasons. For instance, I know my editors and friends over at *The Mac Observer* need to reference some of these reports because the information contained in them might influence the stock markets. If you're a businessperson, some of these reports might pertain to your livelihood, and being able to have easy access to them could help you make better or faster decisions. Of course, if you're a numbers junkie, you might want to follow them just because.

So what kind of reports can you find in Economy? One example is the Manufacturers' New Orders: Durable Goods report, which is published by the U.S. Department of Commerce (actually, it's compiled by the Census Bureau, which is part of the Commerce Department). This report is updated monthly and measures orders received by U.S. manufacturers for durable goods, which include major appliances, cars, and so on. This report is considered a key indicator of how the economy is doing.

Other reports are about industrial capacity, car sales, light truck sales, and more. The app includes several reports on employment, two charts for the U.S. national debt (a Gross report — and it *is* gross, as you can see in the figure on the left, which includes a chart showing the annual deficit or surplus going back to 1949), five reports on the Gross Domestic Product (GDP), reports on the housing sector, inflation, interest rates, and something called Money Aggregates that shows how much money is doing its thing in the economy. That's not all; there are also another 11 or so reports dealing with trade between the U.S., Mexico, and Canada.

If you press the Help button on any individual report — I used the Help button for the Gross National Debt report in the figure on the right — you get a page that gives you the history of the report, where the report comes from, and, sometimes, what the report means.

Another interesting feature in the app is the filter on most of the charts that enables you to sort by president. I'm not venturing into politics here, but if politics is your bag, Economy allows you to pin something good or bad on whichever party you want. A second filtering option enables you to view the charts with recessions marked in gray, or you can turn off all the shading information.

One last note, Economy pulls its data via the FRED (Federal Reserve Economic Data) API, which is offered by the St. Louis Federal Reserve. So, the raw report information is made available through this API, and the developers of Economy have taken the data and formatted it nicely for the iPhone.

Best features

I love that Economy offers no-nonsense and quick access to some of the most important economic reports produced in the U.S., many of which can be a hassle to find.

Worst features

I'd like to see an option to look at recent news stories that involve each report, which seems to me to be a no-brainer feature that I hope is added at some point. I'd also like to be able to rotate the reports to (and reformat for) landscape mode.

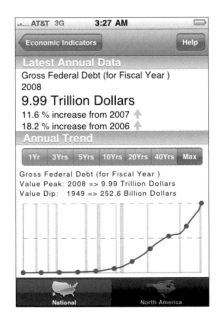

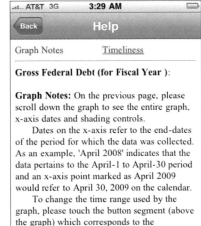

Balance
Free

Balance is a simple and direct ledger app for your iPhone. With it, you can manage an account, easily adding credits and deductions to that account. The entries are easy to make and options are included for naming the type of transaction, how much the transaction is, the date, whether it was paid or received, whether it has cleared, and any notes you want to add. The account can be exported to your Mac or PC as a spreadsheet or as a backup for Balance.

You can make an in-app purchase of a Pro version of Balance that allows you to manage more than one account. The cost for the Pro version is $2.99.

BillMinder (Push)
$0.99 US

BillMinder (Push) is a great app that keeps track of your bills and alerts you when you have a payment due. The *(Push)* in the name means that the app can push those alerts out to you rather than making you check the app. The app exports information as a spreadsheet, has backup options, enables you to mark a bill paid with one tap, and more. Note that if you activate the push capability, you must pay an annual fee in addition to the app price.

Rotate your iPhone when on you're on the Bills tab, and BillMinder gives you a pie chart of all your bills!

iXpenseIt
$4.99 US

This is another really terrific app that tracks your household or business expenses. Each entry has a number of fields you can use, including type, category, and subcategory (for instance Auto as the category and Gasoline as the subcategory), date, vendor, and more. You can

take a picture with your iPhone to attach to the entry. The categories
have icons for easy identification, and you can get several reports
showing you exactly how much you spent, monthly totals and aver-
ages, pie charts, and much more. Your entries are even searchable. If
you want to track your expenses, you'll like this app. There is a free
version (with fewer features) if you want to try before you buy.

Mint.com Personal Finance
Free

Mint.com Personal Finance is another app that ties into an existing
online service. Mint.com is a personal finance site that tracks both
your bank accounts and your expenses. With this app, you can set up
monthly budgets and more. The company's iPhone app enables you to
use your iPhone to see and manage the information in your account.
You can see your account balances, track your monthly income versus
expenses, see your budgets in real-time (handy for knowing how much
you can spend while you're shopping), and even track your retirement
accounts. You can also get monthly reports of your account activity.
If you are a Mint.com user, you'll want this app on your iPhone; and if
you're not, you may want to join Mint.com so you can take advantage
of this excellent free app!

PayPal
Free

If you've ever bought or sold anything on the Internet, you probably
have a PayPal account. With the PayPal iPhone app, you can manage
your account and send money right from your iPhone. You can view
your current PayPal balance, as well as your history filtered by either
sent or received payments (or both). You can see whether a transaction has been completed and what kind of transaction it was (such as
Transfer, Payment, In Progress, and Bill). Sending money is simple, as
long as you have the e-mail address of the account you want to pay.
The only thing you can't do with the PayPal iPhone app is change your
account information.

6 Food, Cooking, and Nutrition

Dinner Spinner (Allrecipes.com)

Free (ad supported)

What's this? A recipe for a salad using beef? That's just crazy, right? I'm the first to admit I wouldn't have readily thought about a salad with beef in it, but Dinner Spinner showed me the light, which you can see in the figure on the left.

Dinner Spinner is a recipe app that ties into the Web site Allrecipes (www. allrecipes.com). It lets you take a slot machine approach to finding recipes, and what could be more fun? Dinner Spinner has three spinning reels, just like a slot machine: In this case, one reel is for the type of dish, one is for the main ingredient, and one is for how long it takes to cook. Shake your iPhone and get recipes matching the criteria that end up on your reels. Sometimes you won't find a match for a particular combination — who knew that dessert recipes pretty much never feature lamb? — but I've found that to be pretty rare so far.

When you hit a combo you like, tap the View Matches! button to be taken to the first recipe that matches your results. For example, you can find 114 main dish recipes for vegetables that can be prepared in 45 minutes or less. And remember those beef salads? You can find 11 matches that can be made in 45 minutes or less. Again, who knew?

Speaking of which, take a look at the figure on the right, which is the very first thing I spun on this app, Chuck Wagon Salad. It's a barbeque beef dish served on a bed of greens. Tap the View This Recipe/Reviews button and you're taken to a page with the name of the recipe and a photograph of the finished dish, an ingredient list, a summary, and a list of step-by-step directions. In short, it's everything you need to follow a recipe.

You can also find nutritional information, including counts for calories, fat, cholesterol, sodium, dietary fiber, and more. This is useful information if you're trying to watch what you eat. Below that are user reviews, which I like because you can't always tell what a dish will really be like from the recipe.

Note that you need a connection to the Internet to use this app. Most of the information isn't stored on your iPhone; instead, it's pulled from the Allrecipes Web site when you need it.

You can obviously lock down one or more of the reels to limit your choices to a specific main ingredient or how long it takes to prepare. You can also manually move the reels to whatever category you want. Either option is convenient for finding a recipe to match what you have on hand, or maybe something you can throw into the slow cooker before you go to work. If the random thing doesn't grab you, you can just search through the recipe list, too.

I've found the app to be most useful, however, when I use the random shake to find new recipes for things I've never even thought about cooking. However you want to use it, it's fun, easy to use, and the recipes are well written and (mostly) easy to follow. I say *mostly* because some recipes are obviously more involved than others.

Best features

This is a great-looking app that is easy to use. The recipes are many and varied, and most of the ones I've cooked have been tasty.

Worst features

Not every recipe on the Allrecipes.com Web site is available in the app. Although I'm not sure exactly how many are in the app, the iTunes description says it has "thousands."

Fast Food Calories Hunter
Free

Do you have a fast food guilty pleasure? Mine is Long John Silver's Chicken Planks. Yeah, that's right, and I'm not (totally) afraid to stand up and admit it, either! They are tasty, especially when dipped in tartar sauce. (Hey, try it before you make that face. It's pretty good.)

Of course, Chicken Planks aren't necessarily all that healthy, but how many delicious things are? The reality is that for decades now many of us have managed to ignore those calorie and fat counts — not to mention the sodium! — but that's been changing in more recent times as fast food chains have begun putting nutritional information in their stores or on their Web sites. It's still been pretty easy to hide from this information, however, even as you're downing another hush puppy.

That is, it *was* easy until the iPhone came out: As Apple says, "There's an app for that." In this case, a little app called Fast Food Calories Hunter offers nutritional information for 67 national and regional fast food chains, as you can see in the figure on the left. It also has basic information on a variety of diets, and a handy Google Maps tool for finding fast food near you.

So take a look at my old friend the Chicken Plank. Turns out that puppy has 140 calories per plank, 8 grams of fat, 20 milligrams of cholesterol, and 480 milligrams of sodium! Ouch! That'll teach me to look this stuff up: I haven't even added in that tartar sauce (100 calories in an ounce, with another 250 milligrams of sodium).

Unfortunately, this is where I have to call a big timeout. It turns out that not all the info in this app is perfectly accurate. For example, as you can see in the figure on the right, Calories Hunter lists the sodium count for that Chicken Plank I keep harping on about in grams, not milligrams. The number is right (480), but the measurement is not. I almost read right over it without noticing it. But of course a single plank doesn't contain 480 *grams* of sodium. That would be like a whole block of salt or something.

So why do I still recommend this app? It's simple: Even if there are some mistakes in the data, the reality is that having all this nutritional information in your pocket makes it easier for you to eat more healthily if you're interested in that sort of thing. For instance, I found that the Chicken Cobb Salad at Long John Silver's has fewer calories; although it's still high in sodium, it's much less than a full Chicken Plank meal. In short, information is power. I just hope the developers get these inconsistencies and mistakes fixed sooner rather than later.

The map feature is another handy aspect of this app, especially when you're traveling, or maybe just away from your regular haunts. Tap the Map button, and you are presented with a Google Maps view of your current location. If you tap the magnifying glass icon, you get a list of the restaurants this app tracks. Choose one, tap the Go button, and all the locations near you appear, represented by a red pin. You can also limit your results to locations that are within two miles, five miles, or ten miles of your location.

Best features

Nutritional information from most of the major fast food chains, all in one convenient source — that's handy!

Worst features

Some of the information isn't right! That would be a deal-killer if it weren't for the overall usefulness of this app.

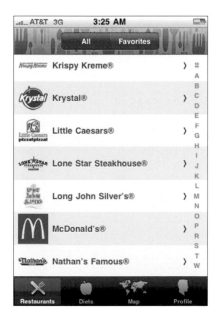
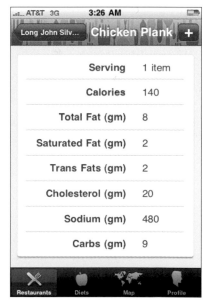

Grocery IQ
$0.99 US

I like to shop. I'm not very organized about it, but I enjoy the experience. About the only thing I *don't* like is when I forget some key ingredient and have to go back for it. Fortunately, I recently discovered Grocery IQ, a shopping list app that is easy to use, supports multiple stores and lists, and has a database of 130,000 items for my shopping convenience.

To start a new list, tap the plus sign (+) button in the List tab, find an item, and you're off to the races. You can add items from your Favorites or History by tapping the Add to List button at the bottom of the item's entry page. In the figure on the left, you see a basic grocery list. Each item on the list is broken down according to the aisle or area in which it's found, which is super-helpful when you have a big list. That way, you can pick up at one time everything located in a certain part of the store.

In my hypothetical shopping trip, I've already gotten eggs, so they were moved to the bottom of the list. See that green bar? It tells me that I have one item in my basket, and that I still have to get four more items. As items you've already gotten are moved out of the way, you have to do less scrolling to look at what you still need to buy, but if you do want to go over what you've already gotten, it's still right there.

When you're finished shopping, just tap the Checkout button and your list is cleared. No muss, no fuss.

Favorites are very handy for those items you often need to add to your shopping list: say, milk, bread, or maybe tuna. (Hey, I told you back in Chapter 5 that I like tuna, and I meant it!) You can add items to your Favorites by tapping the Add to Favorites button on an item's entry page or by going to the Favorites tab, tapping the plus sign (+) button, and doing a search. When you find the item you want, tap it to add it.

The History tab contains everything from your already-completed shopping lists, so that you can easily add them to a new list or to your Favorites. In the figure on the right, items I've put in my Favorites are marked with a star, whereas items already on a current list are marked with a circle. That way, you don't have to go back and forth between tabs to check what you've already put on your list.

Another thing I like about Grocery IQ is the built-in Help feature. When you first open the app or select one of the tabs, a Help pane slides up and tells you how to use whatever you're looking at. It's all pretty simple, but just in case, the Help instructions can explain it to you. Just turn them off by tapping the Don't Show Again button once you know what you're doing.

Have a significant other who can't shop to save his or her life? Make a shopping list and e-mail it to him or her, complete with the proper shopping aisles, and you'll both be happier.

Lastly, Grocery IQ supports multiple lists and multiple stores. It defaults to just Grocery Store, but you can add other stores as you need.

Best features

Grocery IQ is easy to read and easy to use, and setting up a list is fast — especially after you've done a few and have a History and Favorites to work from.

Worst features

The predictive-typing search feature works well, but it's slow.

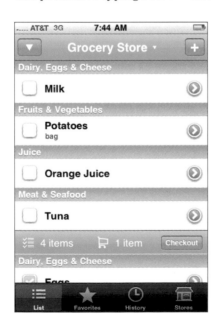
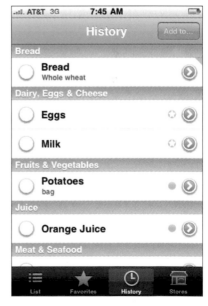

Lose It!
Free

I can't believe this awesome app is free. Lose It! is part calorie-counter, part exercise-measurer, and part coach who knows how much you should be eating and exercising to meet whatever weight loss goal you might have. Lose It! adjusts those levels as you go, without you having to do anything more than enter what you've eaten and how much you've exercised. I used this app for some time, and I found it to be amazingly helpful in monitoring what I eat.

Here's how it works. The Lose It! basic approach is to treat your daily caloric intake as a budget. If you weigh x pounds and exercise y amount and want to lose z pounds per week, you can take in only a particular number of calories to meet that goal. Simple, right? And seemingly obvious, but how many of us manage to follow that simple formula without some kind of help? Yeah, me neither. But Lose It! makes it easy to do just that, which is why I love this app.

To start, enter your weight, your goal weight, and your sex. Next comes your height and your birthday, which is really a polite way of asking for your age because as we get older, our metabolisms slow down. Lastly, the app asks how much weight you want to lose per week.

This is important, by the way, because there's no convincing Lose It! that you can lose 5 pounds a week because . . . well . . . because you can't! Your choices range from ½ pound to 2 pounds per week, but lower goals are more realistic. Oh, and talk to your doctor — a medical doctor, that is, and not Dr. Mac! — before embarking on any program to lose weight.

So, if I enter a current weight of 200 pounds with a goal of 180 pounds, my height and weight, and a plan to lose 1½ pounds per week, Lose It! tells me I can hit my goal in three months and a couple of days. My calorie budget is 1,922 calories per day, which is really a lot of food as long as it's not all chocolate cake and ice cream.

Now that I have my program in place, all I have to do is enter what I eat and how much I exercise. In the figure on the left, you see what I ate for my breakfast, lunch, dinner, and an after-dinner walk I took with my wife. I actually had a few calories left over in my budget as you can see near the top of the screen, which is not unusual. Every day's totals will likely be a little over or under your goals.

What's really handy, though, is that Lose It! remembers these meals under Previous Meals, as you can see in the figure on the right. That's useful because most of us have a lot of repetition in our diet. It makes entering entire meals easy as time goes on.

Also, when you enter a food type, you can specify quantities, and if you're eating something that's not in the database, you can just add your own entry for it.

Foods in the Lose It! database include nutritional info, but you'll have to use the Internet to search for calorie counts if you add a food item yourself. I've been able to find calorie information for just about everything I've looked for, and many national chains even have nutritional information on their sites.

You also log your weight as you go, and, as you lose weight, your calorie budget decreases. That's because, in general, you burn fewer calories when you weigh less. The app does those calculations for you. All you have to do is pay attention to what Lose It! tells you.

I've found that Lose It! makes it easy for me to focus on what I'm eating and how much I'm exercising. That alone may be the killer feature of this app.

Best features

It's easy to use and intuitive, and the database is extensive.

Worst features

The database isn't perfect, however, and I'd prefer not having to search for nutritional information elsewhere and enter it manually.

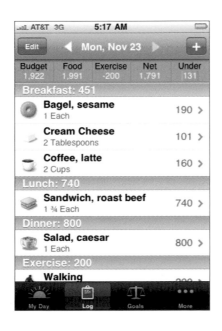

Urbanspoon
Free (ad supported)

This is the big one, right? Urbanspoon was one of the first apps Apple showed in an iPhone app commercial, and what's not to like about an app that can help you pick a restaurant? How many times have you spent 45 minutes playing the "I don't know, where do you want to go?" game with your spouse, your friends, or your workmates? I hate that game, and I can't even begin to tell you how much, but Urbanspoon can change that.

The basic idea of the app is to offer various cuisines, price points, and neighborhoods on slot machine reels. Shake your iPhone (or push the Shake button), and you get a random suggestion for where to eat. If you don't like the result, shake it again. If you want to limit your options, say to a particular neighborhood or a type of food, you can lock the reels.

 Check out the Filter button at the top right of the screen. You can limit your results to Only Popular restaurants and eliminate chains from your results. You can also set a maximum distance and search for specific meals (breakfast, lunch, and so on).

When you get a restaurant you like — Hey look! In the figure on the right, you can see that I got Chuy's, one of my favorite Austin restaurants — just tap the name of the restaurant. In response, you see a screen with the restaurant's address, phone number, the kind of restaurant it is, and a link to read reviews of the place. In the case of Chuy's, you find a critic's review from the *Austin American Statesman*, a blog post that mentions Chuy's, and several Urbanspoon user reviews. There are also buttons for voting on the restaurant with a percentage score of how other users have voted, as you can see in the figure on the right. Very cool!

 If you like or hate a place, make sure to write your own review, and think about the kind of things you find helpful in a review: "THIS PLACE ROCKS!" isn't all that useful.

Back on the main restaurant information page, you can tap the phone number in the listing to call the place. If you tap the address, you are taken to the Google Maps app with that address plugged in so you can get directions.

Now, if you don't want to leave your next meal to the fickle finger of Lady Luck, you can browse Urbanspoon's database by neighborhood, cuisine, features (who delivers?), what's popular, and even by nearby restaurants using your iPhone's GPS and the recently added Scope feature. Tap the Scope button to get a Google Maps page with your location and tons of pins representing nearby restaurants. Tap a pin to find out what it represents. That's pretty cool, in my opinion.

If you're adventuresome, try limiting yourself to one shake and sticking to whatever comes up. It could be awful, but you might also discover a new restaurant you wouldn't have otherwise tried!

Urbanspoon also has a social networking element. You can connect to Facebook (www.facebook.com) to make posts from the app and see your News Feed from others who have also plugged their Facebook info into the app. You don't have to do all that stuff if you don't want to, but it's there. That said, I've noticed that only one of my many Facebook friends has put their info into Urbanspoon.

Best features

I love the Scope feature — it's helped me discover new restaurants that I picked simply because they were close.

Worst features

You need to be connected to the Internet via a cell network or WiFi to use many of the features of this otherwise very cool app. You also won't find every city in Urbanspoon.

170,000 Recipes — BigOven
Free (ad supported)

This app serves as an iPhone-interface for BigOven (www.bigoven.com), a recipe and cuisine Web site. You have to register to use it, but when you do, you get quick access to 170,000 recipes, as long as you have an Internet connection. You can rate each recipe, and there are features like Try Soon Recipes, the Leftover Wizard, What's for Dinner, and the Random Recipe. BigOven has a lot of content, and if you're a foodie already involved in the site, you'll especially like this app.

Note that you can make an in-app purchase for $2.49 to use the app ad-free.

Easy Recipes — Food & Drink
$0.99 US

The Easy Recipes — Food & Drink app has some tasty recipes, including a lot of cocktail recipes, and who doesn't love a good cocktail with their roasted potato wedges? The recipes are divided into eight categories, and they're searchable, too — the Search tab gives you a list of every recipe included, and typing in the Search field filters out only those recipes that contain your search term. This app also has a random feature that returns a random recipe when you make a whisking motion with your iPhone: A simple shake won't cut it. You need the circular flick in your wrist motion!

myStarbucks
Free

One thing I hear all the time is "I can never find a Starbucks when I need one." Okay, I'm kidding. I don't think that phrase has ever been uttered in seriousness, but the company does know how to make a good iPhone app. myStarbucks has a store locator (in either map or list format), a drink builder that shows you what's in all those coffee drinks, information about Starbucks coffee beans and food, and a Favorites function for saving your favorite stores and drinks. Lastly, you can log into Facebook and Twitter (www.twitter.com) through the app to share your Starbucks experiences.

Shopper
$0.99 US

Here's another handy shopping list generator, which is one of the more popular categories in the App Store. With Shopper, you can easily add items from the included database, and all of those items are editable. Shopping lists are presented by aisle, and the aisle information is also editable. There are different categories of lists, and you can specify different stores so each can have its own list. One of the nicest things about Shopper is that it is highly configurable through various options, including the theme, the way lists appear, the ability to designate a default store, and a lot more.

ZAGAT TO GO '09
$9.99 US

If you know and use the ZAGAT restaurant guide, you probably already have this app. If you don't, however, you should probably get it! ZAGAT is one of the most comprehensive restaurant guides on the planet, and the iPhone app gives you access to all 40,000 (as of this writing) restaurant reviews, a GPS-enabled restaurant locator, the capability to search for restaurants according to multiple criteria, as well as restaurant recommendations. This is definitely a must-have app for foodies, and, unlike a printed guide, the app is constantly updated with new reviews. The only caveat is that there are fewer listings for smaller cities and towns, so if you live far from a big city, this app may not be worth ten bucks.

Note that you need a connection to the Internet to use this app because it pulls reviews from the company's servers.

7 Games

The Deep Pinball

$0.99 US

I own half a dozen iPhone pinball games, and the one I enjoy the most and find has the most replay value is The Deep Pinball.

TIP

Before The Deep Pinball came out, its developer's first release, Wild West Pinball (99¢), was my favorite pinball app and is still a close second.

Good pinball games require supremely realistic physics and The Deep Pinball nails it. The way the ball moves around the table and interacts with bumpers and flippers is completely realistic and authentic. So realistic, in fact, that you can "shake" the table to influence the ball's movement. And like a real pinball machine, if you shake too hard, you'll tilt and lose your ball. Furthermore, I sometimes get so involved in my game that I use body English, thrusting a hip or shoulder forward as I shake my iPhone, which my wife finds hysterically funny.

Another hallmark of a great pinball game is great sound effects, and The Deep Pinball doesn't disappoint. The sounds the ball makes when it bounces off a bumper, is hit with a flipper, or passes through a roll-over, are spot-on and totally authentic.

One thing I hate about some pinball games is that they don't let you know your current objective, what happens when you hit specific targets or rollovers, or what targets you should be aiming for right now. The Deep Pinball deals with that by offering a tutorial when you launch the game. It explains your objectives and offers detailed advice about specific features of the table such as the sunken boat, as shown in the figure on the left. Without this tutorial, I might have never realized that switching off the whirlpool opened up access to the sunken ship.

One thing that takes some getting used to is the moving camera used by the game. Although it occasionally pulls back to reveal the entire table at once, as shown in the figure on the right, most of the time, it's zoomed in on the action and following the ball while showing only part of the table. It's similar to what you see in the figure on the left, and I found it disconcerting at first. Fortunately, the game has been updated and you now have a choice of using a "live" (zooming and moving) or "fixed" (see the whole table at once) camera.

Although this game only costs a buck, a free version is also available. It's called (what else?) The Deep Pinball Free. It only gives you one ball and won't save your high scores. But if you just want to see if you like playing pinball on your iPhone and don't want to risk even a buck, you should definitely give it a try.

Best features

Great ball and table physics combined with killer sound effects make for a thoroughly enjoyable and realistic pinball simulation.

Worst features

It can get a bit repetitive with only one table (some pinball games have as many as four different tables).

 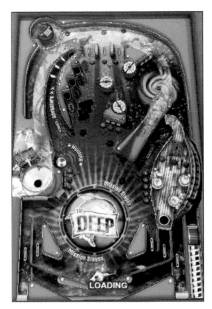

Real Racing
$4.99 US

Dozens of car race games are available for the iPhone, but Real Racing is the real deal. With 48 cars in 4 classes, 12 tracks, and 5 unique game modes, a career mode with 3 divisions and 76 events, plus multiplayer Wi-Fi support for as many as 6 racers, it'll take you a good long time to master it. Heck, it'll take you a good long time to unlock all the different tracks and cars, let alone master it!

One thing I really like about Real Racing is that, unlike many other racing games, it offers a myriad of options for controlling your race-car. You can steer by accelerometer (tilting the iPhone) or by touching the left or right side of the screen. You can accelerate either automatically or manually. And you can adjust the accelerometer and brake sensitivity. Because you can fine-tune these controls, playing Real Racing is a lot more fun than playing other games that offer fewer control options.

Another thing I like is the number of game-play options. For example, if you like racing against real people, you can compete against up to five friends over Wi-Fi. Or you can participate in one of the online leagues and advance to a higher division if you're any good. I think it's cool that league play is open only to players after they've achieved some measure of success in their Real Racing career, so there aren't a lot of novices. This makes league play more enjoyable and challenging.

If you don't want to race real humans, there is still a race mode for every occasion. If you've only got a few minutes, try a three-lap Quick Race against five computer-controlled drivers. Or choose to compete in a Time Trial, where your only opponent is the ticking clock. Finally, there's the career mode, which is guaranteed to take you a long time to complete, with its 76 events. With new tracks and new cars that you unlock when you win, there's always something new and you never get bored.

As you race, you can choose from two different views: the cockpit view, as shown in the figure, or an external "eagle eye" camera view, which follows your car from slightly behind and above it. And unlike some games, Real Racing allows you to switch views during races with a single tap.

The sound effects are great; the tracks are unique; and there are a variety of different driving surfaces such as asphalt, grass, gravel, and ripple-strips, each with its own effect on your car's speed and handling. The driving experience is quite realistic. A good example is that when you tap the brake, your car slows down, but it also downshifts to a lower gear and handles a little better.

One quick tap right before a sharp turn or chicane is better than pressing and holding or multiple taps of the brakes.

I recommended Real Racing when it first came out and was priced at ten bucks. At $4.99, it's a steal. Just check out some of its reviews in the App Store. There must be a good reason for its 4.5 out of 5 star rating and thousands of positive reviews.

And best of all, there's a free version with only one car called Real Racing GTI, so you can give it a try without risking a dime.

Best features

The best thing about Real Racing is that it delivers a lot of variety in its control options, tracks, cars, and race modes against both computer and real opponents.

Worst features

Occasional network errors can spoil online races.

Rock Band

$9.99 US

Let me just start by saying that I think Rock Band is by far the best of the tap-to-the-beat style games available on the iPhone today. Don't get me wrong — I mean no disrespect to the other tap-to-music games, including the tapulous offerings such as Tap Tap Revenge 3 ($0.99), Nine Inch Nails Revenge ($4.99), Metallica Revenge ($4.99), Dave Matthews Band Revenge ($4.99), Lady Gaga Revenge ($4.99), and Coldplay Revenge ($4.99); Gameloft's Guitar Rock Tour and Guitar Rock Tour 2 ($2.99 and $4.99, respectively); Epic Tilt's TapStar Premium ($0.99); or any of the other games in this genre. The fact is that none of those games are bad. In fact, most of them are pretty good, and I was happy to play them until Rock Band arrived on the scene last winter.

Simply put, Rock Band is the most polished, most playable, most flexible, most enjoyable game of them all. And, at least in my opinion, it includes the best songs and has more great songs available for in-app purchase.

On the other hand, if you are somewhat price-sensitive, you may be happy with one of the 99¢ offerings. They're not as good or as much fun, but they are one-tenth the price of Rock Band.

You can play Rock Band solo or jam with up to three other band-mates over Bluetooth. You can play guitar, bass, drums, or even vocals. And you can choose from three levels of difficulty: Easy, Medium, or Difficult (which I think of as insanely, ridiculously, and massively hard, and my son calls, "not particularly tough").

Explaining how the game is played is beyond the purview of this brief essay, but in a nutshell, you tap in the proper place at the right time to score points. The more successful taps you make in a row, the more points you get. If you've played Rock Band or Guitar Hero on an Xbox 360, PlayStation 3, or Wii, you know the drill. The figure on the left is what you see if you choose to play the guitar or bass; the figure on the right is how it looks when you choose vocals.

The game comes with twenty songs, including "Hanging on the Telephone" (Blondie), "Simple Man" (Lynyrd Skynyrd), "We Got the Beat" (The Go-Go's), "Hymn 43" (Jethro Tull), plus songs by Blink-182,

Smashing Pumpkins, Joan Jett, Motörhead, the Pixies, Steve Miller Band, and many more. When you master all these songs (good luck), you can purchase additional songs by Lenny Kravitz, Social Distortion, Devo, and others in two-packs for 99¢.

One of the biggest differences between this game and others like it is that in the other games, the sound doesn't change if you miss a note. In Rock Band, you hear a distinct clunk and the instrument (or vocal) drops out of the mix, which makes Rock Band feel more authentic and truer to the Xbox/PlayStation/Wii games.

Best features

Rock Band plays and sounds just like the console versions of Rock Band and Guitar Hero.

Worst features

For me, the biggest letdown is that, unlike the console versions of Rock Band, you don't actually sing in this iPhone game. Although you can choose to play as the vocalist, instead of singing, you tap the screen. I suppose that's good for the people around you when you're playing, but I found it disappointing.

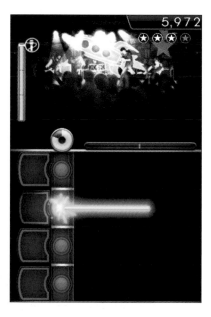

Tiger Woods PGA Tour
$9.99 US

I loved the Electronic Arts Mac version of Tiger Woods PGA Tour and played it until my fingers bled. I love the iPhone version almost as much.

The graphics and level of detail are incredible, as good as I've ever seen in an iPhone game, as you can see in the figure. Notice all the information the screen offers, while at the same time providing a beautifully detailed view of the fairway. Here's what it all means (moving clockwise from top left):

- **Top Left:** Golfer name and bankroll

- **Top Center:** Wind speed (6 mph) and direction (silver triangular "tail" on the "6")

- **Top Center:** Optimal swing strength (94%) and elevation (landing area 1 yard lower than the tee box you're hitting from)

- **Top Right:** Hole number and par for hole

- **Bottom Right:** Where you are (tee) and your lie (100% = perfect)

- **Bottom Right:** Show overhead view (circle that looks like a target)

- **Bottom Center:** Show swing meter (little golfer silhouette in circle)

- **Bottom Left:** Distance to hole (383 YDS); Swing type (Full in this picture; other types include Flop, Chip, and Putt); and club selected (3 Wood).

The user interface is fantastic, and the touch-and-drag swing system is a brilliant example of designing controls specifically for the touch screen. First of all, it requires the proper up and down rhythm and speed. You can make the ball hook or slice by curving your upward swipe to the left or right. And when the ball is in the air, you can put spin on it by swiping madly across the screen in the direction you want the ball to spin. It's easy to master and makes you feel you can hit the ball quite accurately. And most of the time, you can, which makes it a lot like real golf.

Putting is also nicely designed. Your caddy gives you tips that can help you putt more accurately and there's also a "caddy cam" that shows exactly where your putt is going to go. You have to be careful when you use it, however, because you only get to use it once per green.

The game includes seven world-famous golf courses, including Pebble Beach, TPC Sawgrass, and St. Andrews, and you can visit the in-game pro shop to purchase additional courses, including Hazeltine National Golf Club, for 99¢ each.

You can play as a top golfer such as Annika Sorenstam, Vijay Singh, and, of course, Tiger Woods, or just be yourself. And you can use the money you win in tournaments to purchase better golf gear that can give you more power, better control over spin, drives, or putts, improved approach shots, and so on.

While the real-time play-by-play commentary by former pro golfer Sam Torrance and the Golf Channel's Kelly Tilghman adds a certain sense of drama, it also gets a bit repetitive after you've played 30 or 40 rounds. Fortunately, you can control the volume of the commentary, sound effects, and music.

If you like golf or just enjoy a beautifully designed iPhone game, Tiger Woods PGA Tour is a bargain at $9.99.

Best features

Tiger Woods PGA Tour is not only a lot of fun, but it has superb graphics and audio, as well as one of the finest touch screen game interfaces ever. It's easy to learn and difficult to master, which is just the way a game should be.

Worst features

If you quit in the middle of a round, the game sometimes fails to record your score for the last hole you played.

WordsWorth
$1.99 US

As a writer, I love a good word game, and one of my favorites is WordsWorth. In this game, you form words by tapping letters on the screen or dragging your finger through letters to spell a word. Longer words using rare letters such as *J, Z,* and *Qu,* score more points than shorter words with more common letters, such as *A, E,* and *O).* There is also a bonus buzzword at the bottom of the screen in a yellow starburst, like *ska* in the figure on the left or *yin* in the figure on the right. Spelling a buzzword scores a lot more points than the word's usual value. For example, because *ska* and *yin* are buzzwords in the figures, they're worth a whopping 536 and 736 points, respectively. If they weren't buzzwords, neither would be worth more than about 200–250 points.

To make things interesting, special tiles including blue wild cards, green bonuses, and red timers all appear, as shown in the figure on the left. The timer tiles are the most insidious; if the clock runs down before you've used the letter, you lose.

WordsWorth has two game modes. The original (Classic) mode doesn't have a fixed time limit. Instead, it's level-based — each time you achieve the prescribed number of points, you advance to the next level. And, of course, the levels grow increasingly harder with more timed tiles, fewer vowels, fewer wild cards, and more hard-to-use consonants (such as *z, x,* and *q*).

The timed mode gives you a fixed length of time to finish each level. If you don't score enough points to advance to the next level before time runs out, you lose.

In either mode, if you can't find any more words on the screen, you can shuffle the tiles by shaking your iPhone or tapping the little dude at the bottom left corner of the screen. But be careful; only a limited number of shuffles are available for each level, and using a shuffle almost always generates at least one timer tile and sometimes more than one.

The game has numerous options that let you increase or decrease its difficulty. You can choose grid sizes from 4 x 4 to 7 x 7. The figure on the left shows a 7 x 7 grid; the figure on the right is 4 x 4. You can also select a minimum word size (3, 4, or 5 letters), number of scrambles available per level (0, 1, 2, or 3), timer length (10–90 seconds), and word list dictionary the game uses (TWL, SOWPODS, or ENABLE).

Although WordsWorth is simple, it's engaging and addictive. But don't take my word for it. Although it only costs $1.99, a free version also exists — WordsWorth Lite — so you can try it before you buy the full game. Both versions are the same in every way except the Lite version is limited to three levels, versus twenty in the paid version.

I'd be remiss if I didn't point out that there are a lot of terrific word-based games available for the iPhone. A couple of others you might enjoy are Wurdle ($1.99) and WordFu ($0.99).

Best features

WordsWorth is easy to learn, difficult to master, and extremely addicting. And if you have to quit in the middle of a game, you can pick up where you left off the next time you play.

Worst features

None. I've wasted an awful lot of time playing this game and I don't have a single complaint.

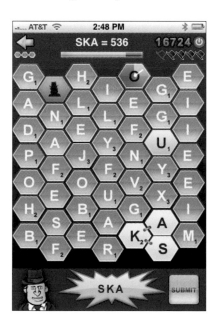
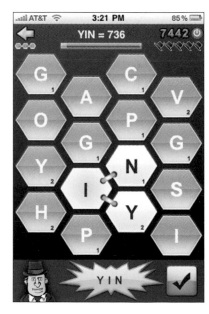

Eliminate Pro
Free

Eliminate Pro is a really good multiplayer first-person shooter. The graphics are excellent and the storyline is engaging. It has numerous unique arenas, each with a different look and terrain, plus a wide variety of weapons and armor, and power-ups galore in every arena. You can challenge friends via Push Notification and they can join your game with a single tap. You can play alone against robots, or use the built-in matchmaking system to find opponents over 3G or Wi-Fi.

The good news: It's free. The bad news: Upgrades take a long time to earn but are available for in-game purchase at prices ranging from reasonable to ridiculous.

iShoot
$1.99 US

iShoot is your classic tank versus tank game with more than 30 different weapons including shells, missiles, cluster bombs, and nukes. Battling on beautiful photorealistic landscapes, iShoot can be played alone (against the computer), by two to four people over a Wi-Fi network, or by two people via pass-the-iPhone style "hot seat" play. It offers a rule editor and a weapons editor that allows you to tweak the game parameters to your satisfaction. It's a lot of fun for less than two bucks.

If two bucks is too much to risk, check out iShoot Lite, a free version with fewer weapons (6 out of 25) and no photorealistic landscapes.

JellyCar 2
$0.99 US

JellyCar 2 is a puzzle game with more than 30 devious levels and 3 modes of play. The object is to guide a squishy car (hence the title) over ramps, wheels, levers, and other obstacles to reach the exit to the next level. It offers great game physics and a playful hand-drawn look, but it's hard to explain in 100 words. Just trust me on this one: It's totally addictive and lots of fun to play. There is no free version to try, but it only costs 99¢ and is made by Disney Interactive. 'Nuff said.

The Secret of Monkey Island Special Edition
$7.99 US

If you were a computer gamer in the early '90s, you probably have fond memories of playing The Secret of Monkey Island from George Lucas's LucasArts game company. The iPhone Special Edition is a faithful re-creation of that '90s classic, which follows the humorous swashbuckling misadventures of wannabe pirate Guybrush Threepwood as he attempts to become the most infamous pirate in the Caribbean. After nearly 20 years, the dialogue has lost none of its wit and the artwork has lost none of its snarky charm. If you liked it back then (or even if you weren't born back then), it's a unique and enjoyable iPhone game.

 ## Trivial Pursuit
$4.99 US

If you've ever played the Trivial Pursuit board game, the iPhone version is a lot like the original, with thousands of different questions in six categories: Arts & Literature, Geography, Sports & Leisure, History, Entertainment, and Science & Nature. The big differences are that it's an app, it fits in your pocket, it doesn't have a game board or tiny plastic pieces to lose, and it only costs five bucks.

It has great graphics and challenging questions and you can play alone or with up to four players via Pass 'N' Play or Wi-Fi.

8 Healthcare and Fitness

 Eight Glasses a Day
$0.99 US

Do you drink enough water? The fact is that most of us live in at least a somewhat dehydrated state. All those sodas and other sugary drinks (did you know that "drink" or "cocktail" in a juice product's name means that it has sugar or corn syrup added to it? It's disgusting!) does not a properly hydrated person make.

I found all kinds of information about this on the Internet. Not drinking enough water can lead to excess body fat build-up, keep your organs from functioning properly, and, for a bit of irony, even cause you to retain water. Not drinking enough water when you're trying to lose weight can supposedly even make it harder because your body can't metabolize fat as fast as it could if you were. So, drink enough water and get a faster metabolism.

 This seems like a good time to insert my reminder that despite being called Dr. Mac, I am not a medical doctor! That means that as smart as I am, you should discuss things like how much water you should be drinking or any kind of exercise program with your *other* doctor, the one with M.D. after his or her name.

So back to the issue of actually drinking all this water! How much should you be drinking? A normal, healthy person should be drinking eight glasses of eight ounces of water per day. I found some sources that suggested that you should add another eight ounces of water for every 25 pounds above your ideal weight you're carrying around. For me, that probably means I should be drinking nine glasses of water.

Great! Now that you know this, it should be an easy matter of just doing it, right? Well, if drinking this much water represents a change in lIfestyle for you, you're probably going to need some help remembering how much water you've drunk from day to day, and that's where Eight Glasses a Day comes in. This is a super-simple app that displays a table with eight full glasses of water. When you drink a glass in real life, tap the virtual glass and watch it empty. In the figure on the left, you'll see that I've been a good boy and drank half my water for the day. When you're done, the screen changes to a congratulatory message and you can tap Start Over the next day.

"But Dr. Mac," I can hear you asking, "you said you need nine glasses a day, and I'll be honest, maybe I should be drinking nine, too. What good is this app for me?" Did you think Dr. Mac would steer you wrong? Nonsense! Eight Glasses a Day can be set to track from one to twelve glasses per day, as you can see in the figure on the right below. You can also set it to automatically start over at 12 a.m. and to show you your remaining count in the app icon. I recommend doing that because it becomes a reminder to drink some water whenever you see the app on your iPhone.

Eight Glasses a Day is a simple app for a simple task, but a task that many of us find hard to do and hard to track. As it might make a significant difference in your overall health, give it a try.

Best features

What I like about this app is its pure simplicity. It literally could not be any easier to track your water consumption.

Worst features

It costs 99¢, which is a lot in the App Store ecosystem for such a simple app, but the benefits of helping you drink enough water are worth a lot more than a buck.

iExercise
$1.99 US

You know, if Apple made a nickel every time someone put an "i" in front of a product name, Steve Jobs would be a rich man. Oh, right, he *is* a rich man. In any event, here we have an exercise tracking app that is, fittingly, called iExercise. This app takes the approach of measuring how many calories you want to burn from exercising, how far you want to walk or run, or how long you want to work out. This is a bit different from the approach of Lose It!, which I talk about in Chapter 6, but that's one of the great things about having all these apps: Somewhere out there is probably an app that does what it does in the way that you want to do it.

One of the things I like most about iExercise is the interface. It's well designed with easy-to-look-at graphics and colors. I'm a sucker for a well-designed interface, and this one definitely qualifies.

In the figure on the left, you'll see the main screen. This is your gateway to monitoring everything you've already done this week and to adding new exercise time. You'll see that I burned 684 calories by exercising compared to my goal of working off 1,000 calories, that I've logged 1 hour and 27 minutes, 3 minutes shy of my goal, and that I've walked 4.7 miles, just a little shy of my weekly goal of 5 miles. It looks like another walk or two, or maybe mowing the lawn, will push me over the finish line. (Okay, so I cheated a bit, and I mowed the lawn before I sat down to write up this app.)

To enter an exercise, tap the Add Exercise button. There's a fairly comprehensive list of exercise activities, everything from a treadmill run to playing soccer to mowing the lawn. I chose mowing the lawn, and on the next screen entered how many minutes it took me (31 minutes today). That brings me to the burger tab you can see in the figure on the right, where you enter calories. iExercise works by doing the calculations for you based on its own internal algorithms, but you can adjust that if you somehow know better. It's too easy to cheat there, so I recommend leaving the calories consumed to wherever it defaults. After you save your information, you're taken back to an updated main screen.

Other features of iExercise include a super cool Achievements screen where you can see various feats you might have accomplished. For instance, if you're a cyclist, you'll get an Achievement for your first

1,000 calorie ride (on up) and there are achievements for burning X amount of fat. Runners and cyclists get Achievements for how far they've traveled in total (like, "Traveled Across Oahu — 44 Miles") and for individual events (like your first marathon or your first half-century ride). Achievements are doled out by the app, and the only way to cheat is to fake an entry, so when you hit an Achievement, I bet it feels good. I say "I bet it feels good" because I haven't yet hit an achievement, but I'm working on it!

All your entries are editable, and iExercise tweets your daily accomplishments and Achievements if you enter your Twitter information. It also tracks your weight and gives you a graph of your progress as time goes on.

Best features

iExercise is easy to use and has a great interface.

Worst features

You can only enter your weight for today, so there's no way to enter your weight from the past if, say, you were tracking your weight before you bought the app. The app could also use a metric option for those living in metric countries.

iTreadmill: Pedometer Ultra with PocketStep
$0.99 US

This is a great app! The developers bill iTreadmill as a "virtual treadmill," but it would be more accurate to think of it as a very capable pedometer. Now, I've gotten a few blank looks when talking to people about a pedometer, so let me explain it right from the top: A *pedometer* is a device that measures your steps when you're walking or running.

iTreadmill measures your steps with your iPhone by interpolating the accelerometer data from your phone. This is awesome if you're into running or walking because it's one less device you have to carry!

The app measures distance, time, pace, speed, calories, step count, and strike rate, and it can display any five of these at the same time. In the figure on the left, I've got it in the default configuration of showing my time up top. Time is repeated below, but each of these displays rotates through the seven parameters with a tap, making the display entirely customizable to your needs. That's a nice touch.

If you're really serious about measuring your walking or running distance more precisely, you should calibrate iTreadmill to your stride. Just tap the Cal button on the Treadmill tab for directions. This involves using the app while you walk or run a specific number of feet (about three miles, and it's different for walking and running).

In addition to measuring your pace, iTreadmill also gives you a beat to help you hit a certain pace. In the figure on the right, I've touched the virtual scroll wheel control to the right of the main display button, and that allows me to set my target speed (you can change it to metric kilometers in the Settings tab, where there's also a setting for changing it to target pace instead of speed). Now, when I tap the Play button, in addition to measuring my steps, it plays a click sound for how fast I should be walking or running to hit the pace I want to maintain.

If you like listening to music when you're walking or running, but you also want help setting your pace, you can turn off all the sounds and just reference the light around the Pacer display. Your mileage will vary on how well that works — pun intended — but it's a nice option to have.

Other key features of this app include a History tab with all the sessions you've saved (for those who like to track and measure their progress), and the capability to autopause when you stop walking or running, which you can turn off if you want. And if you want to measure your calorie expenditure, enter your weight in the Settings tab.

I tested out the app with it in my hand. If I'm listening to music when I walk, I like to have my iPhone out — I don't know why, maybe it's so I can change the song at a moment's notice. In any event, iTreadmill seemed pretty accurate to me, but the makers said they've also mastered the art of interpolating the accelerometer data when the iPhone is in your pocket (they call it PocketStep) for those who like to tuck their iPhone away when they walk or run.

Best features

iTreadmill offers a great interface, and it's easy to use. If I were a betting man, I'd bet the developers made the app they want to use, which is often the key to good software.

Worst features

There should be some different options for hearing different sounds for the pace. Instead of a click, I'd prefer maybe something like a thump.

WebMD Mobile
Free

Step right up! Step right up! We've got your basic medical information, positively free, positively like having a medical doctor in the palm of your hand! Okay, that last bit may be taking things a bit too far, but WebMD's online database of medical information is fairly extensive, and the company's iPhone app makes accessing that information pretty easy.

WebMD lets you look for information in three basic ways: Symptoms, Treatments, and First Aid. Start with Symptoms. See the naked guy in the figure on the left? He's the launching pad for the Symptoms tab. Tap the part of the body that you have a question about, and you're presented with a screen that lists various symptoms specific to that body part. Choose a symptom, and you're taken to another screen that lists symptoms. This might seem redundant, but if you go back and tap another symptom, you'll see that both symptoms are listed together. This makes it easy to go back and forth between multiple symptoms if needed, and if you want to remove one, tap the red circle with the minus sign in it, and then tap the Delete key.

After you have selected the symptoms you want to look up, just tap the View Possible Causes button below the list and you'll get a new screen with one or more conditions that might cause your symptom (or symptoms, if you've added more than one to your Symptoms list). This isn't a substitute for a doctor's diagnosis, of course, but the information might be helpful to you.

There is also a button for Skin and General, which are two more ways to look up your symptoms and are unrelated to the Ken doll figure. Both buttons take you to a list of symptoms, where you otherwise navigate as above.

Move right along to the Treatments tab. Now, as far as I can tell, this feature could have been called Pharmaceuticals 101. But I guess Treatments sounds better. In any event, WebMD has detailed information about some 200 drugs, including warnings, uses, side effects, precautions, interactions, and overdose information. And when I say detailed, I mean *detailed!* As you can see in the figure on the right, you can even identify a drug by its shape and color, or its imprint. Most of us might never need to be able to do that, but if you do, you'll be glad you had WebMD handy.

The last major feature of this app is the First Aid tab. As you probably already figured out, it has basic first aid information for 30 or so injuries, such as burns, bruises, dizziness, shock, and so on. That information is divided into Self-Care at Home, Medical Treatment, and links to additional online information. The first two explain when you should use either, and how to do so. It's written in easy-to-understand English, and I was impressed with what I read.

Now, hopefully you'll never need the information WebMD offers, which is why this may well be one of those apps you never appreciate (or miss) until and if you do need it.

Best features

Extensive medical information on your iPhone!

Worst features

The Symptoms lookup feature uses a hodgepodge of iPhone interfaces, and I found that to be a little annoying — I've always been a big fan of consistency!

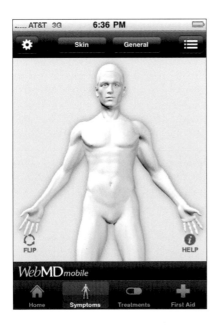

White Noise
$1.99 US

White Noise is one of those apps that you'll really appreciate when you need it. Its raison d'être is to provide background noise for you, something a lot of people want or need when they're going to sleep or just in search of some relaxation.

White Noise offers 40 different sounds, all of which are very high quality samples. That means they sound good, which is important in that making noise is all this app is intended to do. For instance, you have the title track "White Noise," as well as "Brown Noise," "Pink Noise," "Blue Noise," and "Violet Noise," each of which offers a different characteristic to the static sound you might get from a television channel or radio frequency without a broadast.

 If you aren't familiar with the term "white noise," ask your parents. In this age of cable TV and iPods, a lot of young people might never have encountered white noise from an empty channel!

White Noise offers more than just static noise, however; it also includes sounds from the Amazon, ocean and beach noises, crickets, a crackling and popping campfire, several different kinds of rain, a thunderstorm (see below for more information on a dedicated storm version of the app), running water, dripping showers, sprinkler sounds, city noises (which is good for you city slickers on vacation in the country), a dishwasher, a hairdryer, blowing winds, oscillating fans, a wonderful grandfather clock ticking, beautiful chimes, an amazing Tibetan singing bowl, a heartbeat, frogs, a clothes dryer with a quarter bouncing around in it (who could sleep with that going on?!), my wife's favorite, which is a cat purring, and many more. To navigate the sounds, you can either flick with a swipe of your finger, tap the arrow buttons at the top of the screen, as you can see in the image on the left, or see them in list form by tapping the Catalog button.

Each sound comes with an image for quick identification, but that image is static. I wish the app had something more to look at it, but that's just me. Each sound also has a volume slider right there on the screen for making quick adjustments. That's a small touch, but a handy one.

Other features include a timer for turning the sounds off at a specified time or in a specified amount of time, or starting an alarm. The settings also include the capability to have the app quit when the timer is reached, which is very handy for battery life. You can also adjust the left-right balance and the overall pitch of the sound sample. Lastly, there's an ugly digital clock overlay, as you can see in the image on the right.

If you want to try the app, check out the free Lite (ad supported) version that is limited to ten sounds and doesn't have the alarm or favorites toolbar.

If you're a fan of storm noises, there's a version called White Noise Storm for 99¢ that lets you customize your storm! The app offers slider controls for Rain (Distance and Intensity), Thunder (Distance and Frequency), Wind, and a Master slider for overall volume. Unlike the original app, this version also offers some visual effects that match the settings you've chosen, although they're limited to just the top part of the screen.

Try the Random option for White Noise Storm for a storm with changing characteristics.

Best features

Awesome sound samples make these noises sound great through your headphones or the iPhone's internal speaker. I love the Tibetan singing bowl, but my favorite has to be the chimes.

Worst features

The static imagery used for each sound is boring. A video or animated effects would be a nice touch for *watching* the app. The optional clock, while useful, is butt ugly.

BMI Calculator
Free

BMI stands for Body Mass Index, which is a measure of how over- or underweight you are. Enter your height (in centimeters, inches, or feet), your weight (in kilograms, pounds, or stone), your age and sex, and you'll get your BMI. Hypothetically, my BMI is 29.4, which is technically overweight. You should talk to your doctor to find out your ideal BMI, but the point of the app is to allow you to monitor your BMI over time. The app offers a graph of the last ten results, complete with a green, yellow, and red band for understanding where you fall (green is good, red is bad).

Calorie Tracker by
LIVESTRONG.COM
$2.99 US

This is a companion app for LIVESTRONG.COM's The Daily Plate service, which is itself owned by the Lance Armstrong Foundation. With it, you can track your calorie intake from food and your caloric burn from exercises using the LIVESTRONG.COM database of more than 525,000 food and restaurant items, which includes calories and other nutritional information. You don't need an account to access the database or track your activity and food, but you can customize a program and regime if you do. With that account, you can manage your information through the Web site or your iPhone, where it all gets synced.

Eye Glasses
$2.99 US

Eye Glasses is a great app for getting a close-up look at something, which is especially handy for those of us with aging eyes. It only works properly for iPhone 3GS because that iPhone has an autofocus camera. Eye Glasses taps into that camera and its zoom feature (2X, 4X, 6X, or 8X). Just point your iPhone at what you need to look at — say, the small print on a bottle of pills, or maybe the fine print in a legal document — and Eye Glasses shows you a magnified image for easy reading. It's brilliant in its simplicity and utility!

Restaurant Nutrition
Free (ad supported)

Restaurant Nutrition is another handy database of nutritional information for more than 60 national and regional fast food chains in the U.S. Taco Bell, White Castle, California perennial favorite In-N-Out Burger, Chick-Fil-A, A&W . . . they're all here, with many more, and the company adds new chains quite often. You can track what you eat, too, adding items from the database into meals that then go into your history. The app also includes a tie-in to the Google Maps app for quickly finding nearby restaurants from that chain. As of this writing, the developers are planning versions of the app for the U.K. and Canada, and they seem to add new features frequently.

Yoga STRETCH
$0.99 US

Yoga STRETCH is like having a personal yoga instructor in your pocket, sort of. She won't be able to teach you yoga poses you don't already know, but with this app, you can program your own sessions with your own music (or use the default music included), and Yoga STRETCH tells you which stretch to do and when to change. Each pose includes a silhouette of a woman doing the pose against beautiful backgrounds, basic vocal directions on how to do it, along with its English and Sanskrit names, and other information. You can pause your workout, skip poses, or go back to a previous pose as needed.

9 Music

Bloom
$3.99 US

I think what I like best about Bloom is that it's uniquely difficult to describe. That's why I'm leaving the description to its co-creator, ambient music pioneer Brian Eno: "Bloom is an endless music machine, a music box for the 21st century. You can play it, and you can watch it play itself."

Okay. I realize that although that statement does capture the spirit of Bloom, it's not particularly descriptive. So let me try to put it another way. To me, Bloom is one part musical instrument, one part ambient music generator, and one part music-derived art. In its interactive play mode, you tap your iPhone screen to create elaborate musical patterns and uniquely interesting melodies that are paired with colorful patterns of dots that appear when you tap the screen. For example, the figure on the left is what Bloom might look like after you've played it (by tapping) for a few minutes.

Each tap produces notes that sound to me like a 19th century music box mated with a Bösendorfer grand piano to produce a Fender Rhodes electric piano. The three join to sing in unison while random synthesized chord-like structures play softly in the background under the music box/piano tones. At times the chords sound like a string ensemble and at other times they sound like nothing else on earth. I mean that in the nicest way possible.

If you don't feel like tapping, you can let Bloom's generative music player take over to create an infinite selection of compositions with accompanying visuals.

When you launch Bloom, you can select the Classic, Infinite, or Freestyle modes. Each one offers a slightly different kind of audio and video experience. You can also choose to either Listen or Create. In Listen mode, Bloom produces the music for you, although you're free to add your own taps as well; in Create mode, Bloom leaves it to you to do the tapping.

Bloom has myriad settings — some of which appear in the figure on the right — that you can tinker with to subtly alter what you see and hear. The app includes a dozen "moods" to choose from, which are preset combinations of colors and sounds, each with an interesting name such as Neroli, Ambrette, Labdanum, and Tolu.

Bloom is soothing to me, and I often play with it when I'm feeling stressed. If you're a fan of Brian Eno, into meditation, enjoy playing with apps that are soothing and relaxing, or if you just like playing with an interesting app, you'll appreciate Bloom as much as I do.

Best features

Bloom is totally unique and there's nothing else like it except perhaps Trope ($3.99 US) or Air ($1.99 US), which the developers of Bloom also created.

Worst features

It would be nice to have some additional sounds. The music box/Bösendorfer/Rhodes tones are beautiful, but variety is the spice of life. I'd love to hear some other sounds in Bloom.

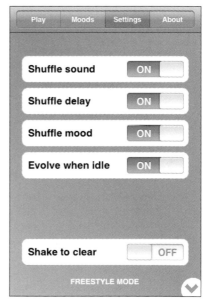

FourTrack
$9.99 US

As a wannabe singer/songwriter, I am in love with FourTrack, an app that turns your iPhone into a genuine four-track audio recorder for less than ten bucks.

If you're familiar with multi-track recording software for your Mac or PC, such as GarageBand, Pro Tools, or Logic, you know what a multi-track recorder does. For the rest of you, a multi-track recorder allows you to record one track, listen to that track while you record another track, listen to those two tracks while you record a third track, and so on.

Here's how I use FourTrack: I choose a tempo and turn on the built-in metronome (*click track*) and then record my acoustic guitar on the first track. When I'm happy with my guitar work, I listen to the first track in my earphones while I sing the lead vocal (melody) and record it on the second track. When I'm happy with the first two tracks, I listen to both of them in my earphones while I sing a harmony or unison (double) vocal part and record it on the third track. And if I'm feeling particularly ambitious, I may even add a second guitar part or a third vocal part on the fourth track.

After I've recorded everything to my satisfaction, I mix the tracks by adjusting the track levels (volume) and pan controls (stereo image left or right). In the figure on the left, track 3 is the loudest and track 2 is the quietest; tracks 1 and 4 are slightly louder than track 2 and a little softer than track 3. The little blue *L*, *C*, and *R* near the bottom of each track indicate the track's pan position. Tracks 1 and 4 sound like they're dead center; track 2 sounds about halfway between the center and left speaker; and track 3 sounds slightly to the right of center.

At this point, I can even enhance the sound of my recording by applying some EQ (equalization), as shown in the figure on the right, or compression. When I'm happy with the way everything sounds, I can use FourTrack's built-in Wi-Fi export to transfer either a stereo mix (all four tracks in a single .WAV file) or four individual tracks (as four individual .WAV files). If I export the individual track files, I can then import them to a desktop audio program such as Pro Tools or GarageBand so that I can continue working on my song.

The sound quality of FourTrack is excellent, and you can make it even better if you use a decent headset or external microphone (such as the Blue Mikey) instead of the iPhone's built-in mic. How good is good? Well, a band called The 88s recorded an entire song called, "Love Is the Thing" using nothing but an iPhone running FourTrack. Visit www.sonomawireworks.com for links to the song and other recordings made by FourTrack users.

I grew up in a time where four-track recording could be accomplished only in recording studios. So FourTrack's audio quality and feature set blow me away. If you sing, write songs, or play any instrument, I feel certain you'll have as much fun as I do creating your own multi-track recordings with FourTrack.

Best features

This app is a freakin' four-track recording studio that costs a mere $10 and requires nothing more than your iPhone. All of its features rock!

Worst features

I wish it were easier to plug an electric guitar or studio microphone into my iPhone. This deficit is actually an iPhone issue, so there's nothing FourTrack can do about it.

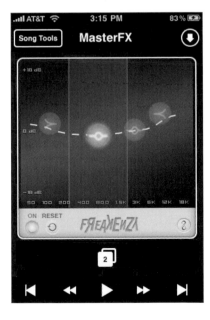

GrooveMaker Free

Free

If you fancy yourself a DJ, freestyle rapper, hip-hop producer, or just someone who likes to create dance/hip-hop/rap beats on the fly, GrooveMaker Free is a superb app that lets you do it right on your iPhone. Using the app is fun; it's easy; and, after you get the hang of it, it's quite addicting.

GrooveMaker Free gives you two free "songs," which in GrooveMaker parlance are remixable groups of audio loops that sound good together.

In the figure, you can see I've started work on a new project. GrooveMaker gives me eight tracks to play with, and I've already filled the first five with

- ✔ A bass loop (Bass) on track 1

- ✔ A random loop (Loop) on track 2

- ✔ A lead line loop (Line) on track 3

- ✔ A sound bed loop (Bd) on track 4

- ✔ A string pad loop (Pad) on track 5

When I tap the Play button near the bottom of the screen (the one marked Groove), these five loops begin to play in unison.

If I tap any of the four Mix buttons on the right side of the screen — Random (D), Inst (C), Perc (B), and Mild (A) — GrooveMaker generates a new mix in the chosen genre by changing the loop(s) on one or more of the tracks. Each time I tap any of the mix buttons I get an entirely new blend of five loops on tracks 1 through 5.

If I tap the Loops button at the bottom of the screen, the Mix buttons are replaced by a long list of available loops. I can replace the loops on tracks 1–5 with different tracks or place new loops on tracks 6–8, which are currently empty.

You can do so much more with this app, but I'm nearly out of space to describe the possibilities. You can adjust the level (volume) and pan (left or right stereo imaging) and Solo or Mute any track. You can save the snippets you build as *grooves*, which you can use as building blocks to create longer *sequences*. Finally, you can export your song as a full quality 44Khz/16-bit .WAV file to share with friends or burn on a CD.

I've been talking about GrooveMaker Free, but you should know that you can also get seven GrooveMaker Style Packs: Club, House, Hip-Hop, Techno, Trance, Drum and Bass, and Electro. You can buy them in the App Store as individual stand-alone apps or as in-app purchases for $4.99 or $9.99 each. That said, you can still have tons of fun and create unique and great-sounding tracks with only the free version and its two free "songs."

One last thing: If this kind of app turns you on, check out the iDrum and Looptastic apps. These are other apps that let you sequence loops and beats. The iDrum series offers loops by recording artists that include Depeche Mode, Ministry of Sound, and RZA of Wu-Tang. Looptastic Producer is a lot like GrooveMaker but, in addition to including six remixable tracks, it lets you import your own AIFF, WAV, or OGG files as loops.

GrooveMaker is truly a remarkable app with a broad and deep feature set. So I urge you to visit the GrooveMaker Web site (http://groovemaker.com) to view the tutorial videos. I guarantee you'll learn some cool tricks that'll help you make better-sounding tracks.

Best features

GrooveMaker has an intuitive user interface and a terrific set of tools. Together they make creating custom musical compositions easy and fun.

Worst features

GrooveMaker doesn't have a way for you to import your own loops.

Leaf Trombone: World Stage
$0.99 US

The description of Leaf Trombone: World Stage in the iTunes App Store says it's "the first massively multiplayer music game." So you're probably wondering why the app is listed here instead of in Chapter 7 with the other games. The answer is that, at least in my humble opinion, Leaf Trombone: World Stage is more like a musical instrument or an episode of *American Idol* than a game.

You can play your Leaf Trombone in one of two ways. The first way requires you to blow into the microphone on your iPhone; the second eschews any blowing. Either way, you tap the right side of the screen to play notes with your Leaf Trombone — tap the long green thing on the right side of the screen in the figure on the left, which I think looks like a kazoo wearing a gold ring. Touch nearer the top of the screen to play lower notes and nearer the bottom of the screen to play higher notes. If you tap, you hear individual notes play one at a time. But when you *slide* your finger up or down the screen you hear the pitch of the note change as you slide — just as if you were playing a real trombone!

When you launch Leaf Trombone, you choose from three options: Play a Song, Free Play, or World Stage. In the Play a Song or Free Play mode you play the Leaf Trombone; in World Stage mode, which I get to shortly, you can play, observe, or judge other performers.

In the Play a Song mode, you pick one of the hundreds of available songs and play along with it. The figure on the right shows a list of my personal favorites. To play the song, you tap the leaves as they move from left to right across the square dots just to the left of the Leaf Trombone itself. When you play the correct note as the leaf passes over the little square, the square illuminates, as shown in the figure on the left.

The songs you play along with are created by Leaf Trombone users with the free Web-based Leaf Trombone Composer tool (`http://leaftrombone.smule.com/composer`).

Free Play mode is like Play a Song mode without leaves or square dots. In other words, you play whatever you please without any accompaniment.

World Stage is the mode that reminds me of *American Idol.* In this mode, you perform and an international jury of your peers judges your performance. If you prefer, you can choose to observe others who are performing and being judged, or you can volunteer to be a judge yourself. Along the way, you earn Achievements (such as Persistent Performer and Expert Judge) and earn rank in both the performer and judge categories.

If you have a friend or family member who has a copy of Leaf Trombone, you can play together in the Bluetooth Duet mode, which doesn't require a Wi-Fi or other Internet connection.

Leaf Trombone is truly one of the most enjoyable iPhone apps I own. If you don't want to shell out a buck, you can go for the free version called Leaf Trombone: Lite & Free. This version limits you to a single song and allows you to observe or judge (but not perform) on the World Stage.

Best features

Because Leaf Trombone includes hundreds of songs and new songs are added every day, using this app never gets old. Judging the Leaf Trombone performances of others may be even more fun than playing the Leaf Trombone.

Worst features

Duet mode is flaky and only works sporadically for me.

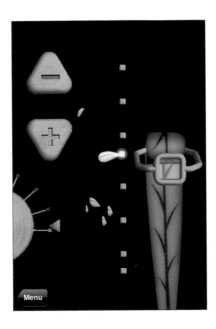
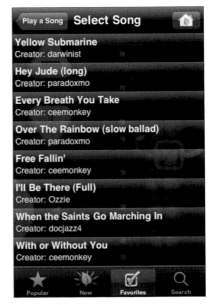

MusicID with Lyrics
$2.99 US

Ever hear a song on the radio, on television, in a store, or at a club and wonder what it's called or who is singing it? With MusicID with Lyrics, you may never wonder again. Just launch the app and point your iPhone's microphone at the source of the music. In a few seconds, the song title, artist's name, and much more magically appear on your iPhone screen, as shown in the figure on the left.

Now, before I tell you any more about MusicID with Lyrics, allow me to provide a little background. Once upon a time, there was a fabulous free app called Shazam that identified songs and artists in the same way as MusicID with Lyrics does. Everyone loved Shazam. My co-author and I even named it one of our ten favorite free apps in *iPhone For Dummies*, 3rd Edition, and said we would happily pay a few bucks for it.

And we would have. The developers got greedy, however, and changed the app's name to Shazam Encore. They began charging $4.99 and crippled the free version by limiting it to a mere five songs per month.

I paid the $4.99 and tried Shazam Encore, which isn't bad. But I then stumbled upon MusicID with Lyrics, which is noticeably better at identifying songs and artists, has a killer feature not available in any version of Shazam, and costs only $2.99.

The killer feature I mentioned is that it offers song lyrics for many of the songs it identifies, as shown in the figure on the right.

If all MusicID with Lyrics could do is hear a song and display its name, recording artist, and lyrics in a few seconds, it would probably be enough to make this a great app. But this app does more, such as providing

- ✔ A link to the song in the iTunes Store
- ✔ A link to related videos on YouTube
- ✔ A biography of the artist
- ✔ A map showing where you were when the song was identified
- ✔ A list of similar songs (with info and lyrics)
- ✔ Identification of songs in your iPod Library (with info and lyrics)
- ✔ Capability to search for songs by title, artist, or lyric phrase
- ✔ Capability for you to e-mail song information to your friends

MusicID with Lyrics is much better than Shazam at identifying classical music, jazz, opera, and show tunes, and it's better at identifying songs by obscure indie bands. I tested MusicID with Lyrics on nearly 100 songs, including the most obscure tunes in my iTunes library, and it correctly identified all but a handful. Furthermore, the songs it missed were really obscure, and it nailed quite a few songs I didn't think it would, such as "In the Court of the Crimson King" by King Crimson; the *Peter Gunn* theme (Emerson, Lake & Palmer live); and songs by the Dave Brubeck Quartet, Dave Clark Five, Dave Matthews Band, David Lee Roth, David Gilmour, David Bowie, and even David Seville and the Chipmunks.

My conclusion is that for popular music, including old and obscure songs, MusicID with Lyrics totally rocks (pun intended) and does a better job than Shazam at identifying jazz, hip-hop, country music, and show tunes.

Best features

MusicID with Lyrics is amazing. It has worked for me in noisy airport terminals, crowded department stores, and even with a DJ at a wedding. This app also makes a jaw-dropping demo of something very cool you can do with your iPhone.

Worst features

Although the app finds the lyrics for many songs, I wish it could find lyrics for even more.

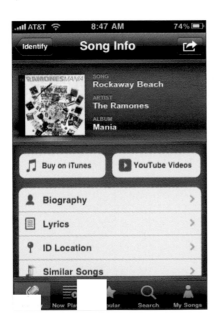

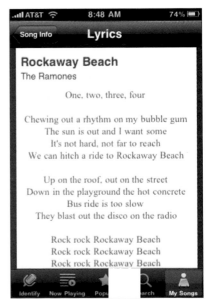

Bebot - Robot Synth
$1.99 US

Bebot is a clever app that's part robot and part polyphonic musical synthesizer. When you touch the screen, the robot moves and makes different sounds controlled by your finger movements. With four-finger multitouch polyphony, multiple synthesis modes, user-definable presets and scales, adjustable synth settings and effects, and more, Bebot is sophisticated but is still simple enough for anyone to use and enjoy.

TIP

If you're a fan of the Beach Boys, select the Theremin preset and see if you can re-create the theremin part in "Good Vibrations." Don't know what a theremin is? Look it up. Don't know what it sounds like? It's the unearthly sound in the choruses and at the end of "Good Vibrations."

Concert Vault
Free

Wolfgang's Concert Vault is an app that provides you with free access to the largest collection of concert recordings in the world. Some of my favorite concerts include The Who, Led Zeppelin, King Crimson, Neil Young, Pink Floyd, Creedence Clearwater Revival, Elvis Costello, and David Bowie. If none of those particular artists appeal to you, you can find concert recordings by hundreds upon hundreds of other artists.

The cool thing about Concert Vault is that it gives you access to exclusive recordings you probably haven't heard before and probably won't hear elsewhere, such as master recordings from the archives of Bill Graham Presents, the *King Biscuit Flower Hour*, and many others.

I Am T-Pain
$2.99 US

Do you know what the Auto-Tune sound is? It's the weirdly altered vocal sound first heard on Cher's 1998 hit, "Believe," and more recently used by R & B singer T-Pain, not to mention most rap and hip-hop songs of recent memory.

With I Am T-Pain you can apply the famous Auto-Tune effect to your voice as you sing along with several of T-Pain's most famous songs, which come complete with lyrics, Auto-Tune settings, and timings. If you prefer, you can freestyle and record your Auto-Tuned voice.

Prices for the Antares Technologies (www.antarestech.com) Auto-Tune plug-in used by the pros start at $129; the I Am T-Pain app costs $2.99 and is almost as much fun. Any questions?

Pandora Radio
Free

Pandora Radio is one of the coolest concepts ever. You tell it the names of your favorite musicians and songs and then Pandora creates an instant personalized radio station that plays only songs that exemplify the style of music represented by the artists and songs you named.

I based one of my Pandora stations on songs by the Byrds, Tom Petty, and the Beatles. The result is a station with songs by those artists but also a lot of similar music by artists with whom I'm not familiar. I made another station based on music by Dave Brubeck that plays great music by jazz artists I've never heard before.

Pandora Radio is free. It's awesome. Give it a try.

Simplify Music 2
$5.99 US

The iPhone is a fabulous iPod, but even the 32GB iPhone 3GS doesn't have enough storage space for all my music. Simplify Music 2 fixes that deficiency by letting me stream all the music in my iTunes library (Mac or PC) and listen to it on my iPhone via any Wi-Fi or 3G cellular connection.

That feature is pretty cool, but what's even better is that you can invite up to 30 of your friends to listen to your entire iTunes music library, and you can listen to the music libraries of up to 30 of your friends, as well!

The more music (and friends with music) you have, the more you'll love Simplify Music 2.

10 Photography

ColorCanvas Plus
$0.99 US

Some photography apps are like a Swiss Army Knife, with bells, whistles, and features galore. Others, such as ColorCanvas Plus and its free sibling ColorCanvas Basic, focus on doing one thing well. In this case, that one thing is converting a photo to black and white and then enabling you to selectively colorize specific parts of it. Because a picture is worth a thousand words, I could technically tell you to check out the before (left) and after (right) pictures and move on to the next app.

Never fear, gentle reader; I vowed to tell you what you need to know. Even though that pair of pix says it all, let me tell you how the app works and how easy it is to achieve stunning effects.

Start with a picture. You can shoot a new one or select it from your iPhone's Camera Roll or Photo Album. Either way, the second step is to choose one of the three mono-color filters — normal, enhanced, or hi-contrast — offered by ColorCanvas Plus. The difference between the three is subtle, and the best way to determine which one is best for a particular image is to try all three.

Now it's time to get creative and break out one of the three brushes, called Color, Mono, and Tint. The Color brush brushes away the black and white to reveal the color from the original photo. The Mono brush does the opposite — it brushes away color you've revealed with the Color brush, which is handy if you make a mistake or want to zoom in to clean up problem areas. Finally, the Tint brush lets you tint any part of the image.

In the picture on the right, I used the color brush to reveal the colors in my daughter's hat, hair, skin, and snake. I accidentally revealed some of her colorful bathing suit top, so I painted over it with the mono brush until it was just right. Finally, I wanted her hat and the snake to stand out a little more, so I carefully tinted her cap a dark shade of blue and tinted the snake with a mustard-like wash.

Your paintbrushes can be any size, from pencil-thin to fatter than my thumb. You can adjust the brush's opacity from nearly transparent to pretty much opaque. Finally, you can undo and redo brush strokes to your heart's content.

The bottom line is that if a talentless clod like me can achieve stunning (in my humble opinion) artistic effects with ColorCanvas Plus, just think what you'll be able to do.

The free version, called ColorCanvas Basic, doesn't include the Tint brush or paint colors, which I think are essential. However, the free app is kind of fun to use if you're too cheap to pay a buck for ColorCanvas Plus.

Best features

With ColorCanvas Plus you can create a unique and interesting effect with little effort or talent.

Worst features

The zooming and panning features don't work as smoothly as in many other apps.

Comic Touch
$2.99 US

You have a phone and the phone has a camera. If you also have a sense of humor, you need Comic Touch, the iPhone app that lets you be a cartoonist even if you can't draw a straight line.

Shoot a new picture or select one from an iPhone Photo Album, and let the fun begin. You can put words in peoples' mouths by adding cartoon balloons in four different styles: Speech, Thought, Whisper, and Exclaim. You can add a caption to describe the scene, give the scene a title, or just add text to make fun of your subject. You can see all of these features in the figure on the left. "Antennas? What antennas?" is a speech balloon; "Jacob was somehow different. . . ." is a caption.

The developers of Comic Touch weren't chintzy, providing you with the tired old Marker Felt font, either. Instead, all your comic words appear in an exclusive comic-lettering font that you won't find in other apps.

Comic Touch couldn't be easier to use. After you select the picture you want to deface, drag cartoon balloons and caption boxes onto it. Double-tap any balloon or caption box to open the app's Details screen, which is where you can type your words, select a font size (Small, Medium, Large, Extra Large, or Giant), and choose a color scheme (black on white as shown on the left, or white on black).

Just for fun, Comic Touch also provides several goofy distortion effects including Bulge, Dent, Stretch, and Light (as shown in the figure on the right). The nifty Smudge tool lets you freely warp images any way you like. If you decide you don't like your smudging, you can shake your iPhone to restore the original image.

When you're happy with your creation, you can save it to your iPhone Camera Roll or e-mail it to friends or photo-sharing sites such as Flickr.com and Skitch.com.

That's about it for features in Comic Touch, so let me give you a couple of tips for using the app effectively. First, go to the Web site (www.plasq.com/comictouch) and watch the movie. It wasn't until I did so that I learned you can delete any balloon or caption by pressing and holding for a few seconds until a little x appears, just like when you press and hold an icon on the iPhone's home screen. Tap the x to delete the balloon or box.

You can also position or reposition any cartoon balloon by pressing in its middle and dragging. You can position the balloon's tail — which is the part that comes out of the person's mouth — by pressing on the tip of the tail and dragging it where you want it.

One last thing: There's a free version of the app called Comic Touch Lite, but it has a reduced feature set and places an ugly watermark on any comics you save or share. *Caveat emptor* (even though it's free).

Best features

I love everything about Comic Touch. I get a lot of laughs putting words in peoples' mouths and then sending them the results. I have more fun with Comic Touch than with almost any other app I own. Every time I send one of my comics to someone who uses an iPhone, the person begs me to tell them what app I used and usually then buys the app and loves it.

Worst features

It would be nice to be able to add borders and create multi-panel comics, just like comics from Marvel and DC. Even though the comic lettering font is unique and good-looking, I'd be happier if I had a few fonts to choose from (there's only the one).

FX Photo Studio
$1.99 US

If you're only going to buy one app to use with your iPhone camera, FX Photo Studio is probably your best bet. With 119 mostly high-quality photographic effects, I don't know of another app that offers as many decent options at any price, let alone one that costs less than 2¢ per effect.

The effects are divided into 14 categories for your convenience: Image Correction (as shown in the figure on the left), Color Fantasy, Texturize, Color Temperature, Overlay, Glow, Hue, Vintage, Simmetry (*sic*), Blur, Distortion, Frames, and Photo Styles.

Each category contains five or ten different effects, including useful ones such as More Contrast, Brighter Image, Less Colors, and Radial Blur. The app offers dozens of artistic effects, such as the Vintage Burnt Paper effect I applied to the picture of myself in the top half of the figure on the right (the bottom half, of course, shows the original image for comparison).

I'd be remiss if I didn't mention that the app includes a number of effects I wouldn't use on my worst enemy, much less someone I like. For example, the Kisses overlay embeds a bright red lipstick print on your photo, whereas the Ghost, Skull, and Scary Face effects stick a stupid-looking semi-transparent ghost, skull, or fanged face, respectively, in your picture. On the other hand, the dumb effects are a small fraction of the total, and most of them aren't nearly so stupid.

After you shoot a new picture or select an existing photo from your iPhone Photo Albums and choose an effect to apply to it, a small preview appears mid-screen. The preview is a nice touch because applying the effect can take a few seconds; after checking out the preview, you can cancel the effect instead of applying it if it's not what you want.

Speaking of processing time, FX Photo Studio lets you choose the resolution for the images you modify — anywhere from 320 to 2048 pixels on an iPhone 3GS (earlier models only allow a max of 1024 pixels). The higher the resolution you select, the longer it takes to apply an effect, which at the highest resolution can take several minutes. The good news is that FX Photo Studio offers an option to display Amazing Facts during image processing such as, "The surface speed record on the moon is 10.56 mph, set by a lunar rover." I found some of the facts quite interesting, and reading them is better than having to stare at a spinning pinwheel for a minute or two.

With all the available effects, you might have a hard time deciding which one to use, so there's a handy die icon. Tap it to see a preview of a random effect. Tap Cancel and tap the die icon again to see a different random effect, or tap Apply to apply the current effect to your image.

FX Photo Studio includes a couple of other nice features in addition to the effects. One is a slide control for adjusting the Gamma (luminance) of your image. Another is a cropping tool that lets you rotate your image in 1° or 5° increments before you crop it.

Finally, you can apply multiple effects to an image and use a multistep undo option if you don't like the results.

Best features

FX Photo Studio offers so many useful and artistic effects there's something in it for everybody. The quality of most effects is quite good. This app is a bargain at $1.99.

Worst features

My only criticism is that misspelling a category name is just sloppy, and *Simmetry* isn't even a real word.

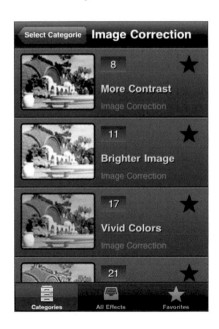

OldBooth Premium
$0.99 US

Have you ever wondered what you might have looked like if you had lived and dressed in the styles of another era? All you need is a copy of the OldBooth Premium app and you won't have to wonder any longer.

OldBooth Premium enables you to take any full-face photo and insert the person's face into hair and wardrobe from another time. This is another case where a picture is worth thousands of words, so take a gander at the figure at the bottom of the next page, which clearly demonstrates just what OldBooth Premium does.

You get the picture, don't you? (Pun completely intended.)

The top row of snapshots shows the original picture of me on the left and three OldBooth-ed versions (left to right): Afro-hair Bob of the sixties, suave Dean Martin-esque Bob of the fifties, and Bob as Steve Jobs in the eighties. Beneath that is an original photo of my wife on the left with three OldBooth-ed renditions of her (left to right): Roaring twenties Lisa, fifties bouffant hair Lisa, and Lisa as a beret-wearing beatnik of the sixties.

Creating one of these goofy portraits with OldBooth Premium is as easy as 1-2-3:

1. **Choose a gender and then select one of the nearly 30 mask styles available for each gender.**

2. **Choose a picture to deface.**

   You can either take a new photo with your iPhone's camera or choose a picture from your iPhone's Photo Library.

3. **Resize the picture by pinching or unpinching, rotate the picture by pressing and dragging, and adjust the brightness of either the picture, the mask, or both. If your original image is facing the wrong way, double tap to flip it horizontally. And if you mess up entirely, triple tap to start over.**

   When you're happy with the image, tap the Done button to save it to your iPhone's Camera Roll, where you can use it as wallpaper, e-mail it to a friend, assign it to a contact, or send it to your MobileMe gallery. Of course, the doctored image is exported to your Mac or PC the next time you sync your iPhone.

OldBooth Premium is simple to use, gives great results with very little work, and is just plain fun. Furthermore, if a buck is more than you want to spend, check out the free version. It's called OldBooth (without the *Premium*), and it only includes a handful of masks for each gender.

There is one last thing . . . OldBooth Premium includes two hidden super-secret masks — one for each gender. The male mask is the Steve Jobs-like one shown on the far right of the top row of pictures. I'll leave it to you to discover the female mask. The secret is to triple tap the words Choose Style on the male or female Choose Style screen.

Best features

You can have a lot of fun disfiguring your friends with OldBooth Premium, and it only takes a couple of minutes to create a pretty good likeness. None of the pictures below took more than two or three minutes. After you get the hang of using OldBooth Premium, you can knock out doctored photos really fast.

Worst features

I'm sick of the masks already. I'd even pay more for a version with new or different masks. That said, I've had this app for more than a year, so it'll take a while before you get sick of them, too.

Photogene
$2.99 US

Photogene is one of my favorite apps. It's the app I use most often when I need to improve a photo I shot with my iPhone. It has most (if not all) the features I need to make a mediocre photo look good or to make a good photo look great.

Photogene has an exceptional user interface with controls that are easier to understand and use than some other photo apps. Photogene also has an extensive list of features, represented by the nine icons on the far left side of the screen (as shown in the figures):

- ✔ **Scissors:** This cropping tool provides several preset aspect ratios, including 1:1 (square), 3:4 and 4:3 (standard rectangular photos), 9:16 (widescreen), and 3:2 (iPhone screen).

- ✔ **Arrows:** This icon has tools for rotating, flipping, or straightening your photo.

- ✔ **Funnel (at least I think that's what it is):** This icon reveals tools for sharpening your photo, turning it into a pencil sketch (as shown in the figure on the right), plus three special effects — sepia tone, night vision, and heat map.

- ✔ **Color wheel:** This icon reveals serious image-editing controls: levels, exposure, colors, and RGB. I love the Photoshop-like histogram for adjusting relative brightness levels, as shown in the figure on the left. Tap the Auto button to the right of the histogram, and Photogene does its best to optimize the levels in your image automatically. It usually does a pretty good job, so I suggest you try the Auto button before you drag the level sliders hither and yon. The exposure control is actually two slider controls — one for exposure and the other for contrast. The colors control is also a pair of sliders— saturation and color temperature. If you drag the saturation slider all the way to the left, it makes your photo black and white. Finally, the RGB balance control has three sliders that let you increase or reduce the red, green, or blue channels in your image.

- ✔ **Star:** This icon enables you to drag a variety of cartoon balloons and shapes onto your photos with complete control over the outline, fill, and text colors. You also have a choice of five fonts (but none look as much like a comic book as the exclusive font used by Comic Touch).

- ✔ **Square:** Tapping this icon (shown in the figure on the right) discloses the frames, backgrounds, and effects options. The tape on the corners of the image is one of the preset frame options; the blue background is one of the background color options; and the reflection below the picture is one of the special effect options.

✔ **Curved arrows:** These two icons let you undo and redo any effects you've applied to the current image. It lets you undo one mistake or even many mistakes. What's really cool about it, though, is that it also lets you see your picture before and after an effect is applied.

✔ **Done:** Tap this check mark icon to save your work after editing.

Best features

All of Photogene's features are really quite excellent, so I think the best thing about this app is that it has so many high-quality image-editing tools. The intuitive and uncluttered user interface and unlimited undo/redo support are not too shabby, either.

Worst features

My big complaint is that the shadow effect options for frames are ugly and there is no way to adjust their transparency.

My minor gripe is that the pencil, reflection, and frame effects work well and deliver beautiful results on most images, but I wish there were more special effects such as crayon, oil paint, mosaic, or watercolor. If those effects existed and looked as good as the pencil, reflection, and most of the frame effects, they'd be awesome!

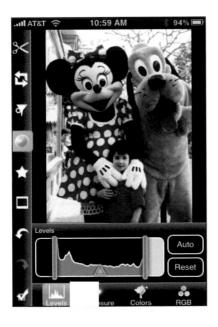

Best Camera
$2.99 US

Inspired by the old saying, "the best camera is the one that's with you," Best Camera was designed by renowned photographer Chase Jarvis. He wanted an app that made it easy to shoot, creatively edit, and share photos. With 14 great-looking effects, previews, selectable resolution, and integration with Facebook, Twitter, and any sharing service that lets you upload pictures by e-mail (such as Flickr.com), if it's not the best, it's still very good.

What makes Best Camera unique is its clever interface, which is designed to let you change the order of the effects after you apply them. You can experiment with Best Camera in ways you can't with other apps by shuffling the order in which the effects are applied.

FocalLab
$0.99 US

Okay, some people might call FocalLab a one-trick pony, and I wouldn't argue. But in the case of this app, the one trick is so cool that it's easily worth a buck to me. FocalLab applies professional-looking depth of field and lens effects to your photos. There are four blur options — dreamy, soft focus, zoom, and motion blur — plus a vignette effect with three shapes, and adjustments for center point and light fall-off. The thing that makes all the effects look so spectacular is a slide control for adjusting the intensity and a feature for "selective focusing," which lets you choose the location and size of the in-focus area.

Pano
$2.99 US

Pano lets you take seamless panoramic pictures with your iPhone. With a handy semi-transparent guide and advanced alignment, blending, and color-correcting algorithms, you can stitch together up to 16 individual photos and save the finished panorama — with a resolution of up to 6,800 x 800 — directly to your iPhone camera roll.

This app is a hoot. The guides make it easy to get exceptional results and the finished product can be spectacular.

Check out the excellent examples of what Pano can do in the Pano for iPhone group at Flickr.com (`www.flickr.com/groups/iphonepanoramas/`).

Photoshop.com Mobile
Free

Another excellent choice for improving photos, Photoshop.com Mobile has all the features you'd expect from an app that bears the Photoshop name — crop, rotate, flip, exposure, saturation, tint, and color-to-black-and-white conversions. I don't much care for the Sketch and Soft Focus filters or the special effects, such as Border, Vignette Blur, Warm Vintage, Rainbow, and Soft Black and White.

Wondering why I recommend it? Well, I really like the way it's integrated with my Photoshop.com account. I can upload to and download from my online photo library and use the much more advanced Photoshop.com image editing tools for images that need more help than any iPhone app can provide.

Reel Director
$7.99 US

Although it's for the iPhone 3GS only, Reel Director is an amazing app that lets you do great things with movies you shoot with your iPhone. It's hard to believe, but Reel Director lets you combine and rearrange clips, add text overlays, add really cool opening and closing credits and title cards, and — my favorite feature — includes 27 really sweet transitions, which have animated previews and can be applied globally to an entire project.

Reel Director isn't Final Cut Pro or even iMovie, but it does let you do amazing things with video using nothing but your iPhone.

11 Productivity

Awesome Note (+Todo)

$3.99 US

The iTunes App Store has more note-taking, to-do list apps than I can count — with more coming out every day. My main app in this category is OmniFocus for the iPhone. But OmniFocus is expensive ($19.99) and really works best if you synchronize it with the OmniFocus desktop app, which is also expensive ($79.95) and not available for Windows. If you're a Mac user and don't mind the high prices, check out both apps. For everyone else there's Awesome Note (+Todo).

I looked at more than a dozen note storing-and-organizing and to-do list apps and I think Awesome Note (+Todo) offers the best combination of features and flexibility for its price. Plus, it's one of the best looking (if not *the* best looking) apps of its type. Its user interface is powerful, yet simple and elegant, as you can see in both figures.

The figure on the left is Awesome Note's main screen. Tap the Quick Memo button to quickly start typing in one of the four sticky note memos. Tap a folder to see a list of the notes it contains (there are four in the Books folder, two in Personal, two in TMO Reviews, and so on). Or tap New Note to start typing a new note item, which you can file in any of your folders. Options for each note include due date, checkbox, priority (0, 1, 2, or 3 stars), font and font size, and a variety of themes, which are pretty background images (chalkboard, stone, pale ivory, and so on) behind the note text.

Due dates for notes are indicated on the folder they're stored in. In the figure on the left, the little numbers in the circles on the TMO Reviews, Shopping, and To-Do List folders indicate that each folder contains one item (note) that's due today.

If you tap in the middle of the screen where it says All Notes 15, you see a list of all the notes in all your folders, displayed by their due dates; the item with the earliest date (Today in the figure on the right below) appears at the top of the list. You can sort the items in each category (Today and Next in the figure) by modification date, creation date, name, due date, or priority.

Other nice features include the capability to protect folders with a four-digit passcode, three views for folder contents (thumbnail, list, and task), an unlimited number of folders and notes, fast global search, and easy import, export, backup, and restore via the free Google Docs service.

Finally, if you're not sure Awesome Note is right for you, download Awesome Note Lite, which is a free version that's the same in every way except that it's limited to seven notes.

Best features

Awesome Note has a beautiful and elegant user interface and is powerful while still being flexible and easy to use. If you don't believe it, try the free Lite version first.

Worst features

Awesome Note doesn't sync with a desktop or Web-based to-do list app.

BargainBin
Free

I'll let you in on a secret: The price of apps isn't set in stone. Developers often reduce the price of apps for a limited time to build some buzz or introduce a new app or feature. The coolest part is that the reduced price is, as often as not, *free*.

You've got to love discounted apps. But here's the rub: With more than 100,000 apps available in the App Store, it's not easy to find the discounted apps using iTunes on your computer or the App Store app on your iPhone. That, gentle reader, is why BargainBin is such a beautiful thing. Not only does it keep track of apps and prices automatically, it can alert you when prices drop. It also does some other things, but finding apps that are currently on sale is its forte.

The figure on the left shows BargainBin's main screen. BargainBin filters apps that are on sale into 20 different categories, including Productivity, Music, and Social Networking. Browse all of the apps on sale in All Categories at once, or browse Popular apps that are on sale. Last, but certainly not least, you can set up a Watch List to keep track of prices for apps you might want to buy if the price goes down.

If you tap any item besides Watch List (see the figure on the left), a list of the apps on sale appears, as shown in the figure on the right. The lists have three buttons — All, Bargain, and Free — near the top of the screen. The All button shows every app that currently has a reduced price or is free; the Bargain button shows only apps with price reductions of 50% or more; and the Free button shows only apps that are free.

If you tap any app in any list, four buttons appear below it:

- **Watch:** Adds the app to your watch list
- **App Store:** Launches the App Store app so you can buy the app or read its reviews (which aren't available in BargainBin)
- **Description:** Displays a description of the app
- **Screenshots:** Displays screen shots of the app

In addition to tracking individual apps on your Watch List, BargainBin can alert you when any app in any category goes on sale or when any popular app goes on sale.

Speaking of alerts, not only can BargainBin watch specific apps for price reductions, it can alert you to price drops. You can choose any or all of three types of alerts: sound alerts, on-screen alerts (such as the ones displayed by the Messages and Phone apps), or badge alerts (those little numbers shown on an app's icon, such as the ones displayed by the Phone, Mail, and Messages apps).

One last thing: Because all the lists in BargainBin feature only apps that are on sale, you'll be happy to know that you can search for any app in the App Store and add it to your Watch List.

Best features

BargainBin has two great features: It alerts you to price reductions, even when the app isn't running, and it simplifies finding apps that are on sale or free.

Worst features

This is more of a missing feature than a bad one, but I would love to get alerts by e-mail, too. I'd also love to see user reviews and ratings.

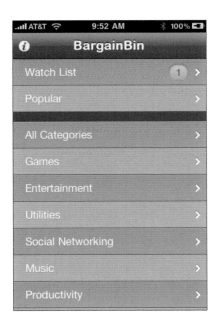

Dropbox
Free

This could get confusing. You see, Dropbox is not only the name of this iPhone app, it's also the name of the company, the name of the service it provides, and the name of the software that runs on your Mac, Windows, or Linux computer. So I'll call the iPhone version *Dropbox iPhone app,* and refer to the other parts as plain ol' *Dropbox.*

I was a huge fan of Dropbox (www.dropbox.com) long before the Dropbox iPhone app came along. To understand the beauty of the Dropbox iPhone app, you first need to know what Dropbox is and how it works.

Dropbox is, in a nutshell, software that syncs your files online and across your computers. You can use it to synchronize files among as many Mac, Windows, or Linux computers as you want. You can use it to share files with anyone you want. And you can use it to back up important documents.

You first create a free Dropbox account and install the free Dropbox software on your computers (let's call them Computer 1 and Computer 2). A folder named (what else) Dropbox appears on each computer and all files you put in the Dropbox folder on Computer 1 are instantly available in the Dropbox folder on Computer 2 and vice versa. Plus, because Dropbox stores those files on its own secure servers you can access them from anywhere with any Web browser.

Whew. Now that you know how the Dropbox system works, I can tell you about the Dropbox iPhone app, which gives you access to files in your Dropbox folder(s) from your iPhone.

With the Dropbox iPhone app, you can use the Internet connection on your iPhone to view the files in your computer's Dropbox folder, as shown in the figure on the left. You can also specify "favorite" files that are automatically copied to your iPhone so that you can access them without an Internet connection, and you can e-mail links to files in your Dropbox so your friends can download them.

Wondering what kind of files you can view in the Dropbox app? Well, you can view all the usual suspects: Microsoft Office (Word, Excel, and PowerPoint) files; Apple iWork (Pages, Numbers, and Keynote) files; .PDF files; most types of image files such as (but not limited to) .JPEG, .TIFF, and .PNG; as well as music and video files. You can also upload photos or movies (iPhone 3GS only) from your iPhone to your Dropbox folder.

Speaking of image files, whenever you have pictures in a folder that's in your Dropbox folder, the pictures magically appear on your iPhone screen as photo galleries, as shown in the figure on the right.

I love Dropbox. Let me tell you a few of the ways I use it. I use it for current projects so I have access to those files from any computer in the world, as well as from my iPhone. Because the files are stored on the secure Dropbox server, they serve as an up-to-the-minute backup of my files. Finally, whenever I travel, I put my best photos into a shared Dropbox folder so my friends and family can enjoy them at their convenience.

Best features

Free app with 2GB of free online storage that you can use any way you like.

Worst features

You can't zoom in or out of graphics files (although you can for other file types). Unlike Dropbox on a computer, you can't share links to folders; the iPhone app only sends links to individual files (but not folders).

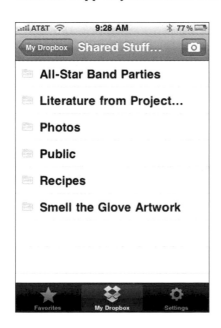

Pzizz Relax
$2.99 US

I've come to believe that taking a 15- or 20-minute power nap during a long workday helps rejuvenate and revitalize me. That being said, I didn't take many power naps until I discovered Pzizz Energizer, a revolutionary little program (available for both Mac and Windows; www.pzizz.com) that combines several different techniques to help me power nap and recharge my batteries. I was thrilled to hear that the Pzizz folks had introduced an iPhone app called Pzizz Relax, which uses the same technology and principles as the Mac software. Now all I need is my iPhone and some earphones to power nap anywhere I want at any time I choose.

According to its inventors, Pzizz Relax "combines Neuro Linguistic Programming (NLP) techniques, specially composed music, sound effects, and a binaural beat to induce a wonderfully relaxed state, similar to that of the Rapid Eye Movement (REM) stage of sleep." They claim that listening to this combination of sounds encourages us sub-consciously to relax, focus, and energize the body and the mind.

The whole thing sounded like hokum to me, but I'll try almost anything once. I was extremely surprised to discover that Pzizz Energizer (the computer version of Pzizz) worked for me — after my very first Pzizz power nap I felt relaxed and refreshed. In fact, I try to grab at least one 10- or 15-minute Pzizz nap every afternoon.

Pzizz Relax gives you complete control over what you hear. You can turn its guiding voice, suggestions, and 3-D audio on or off for any nap. You can adjust the music and voice volume levels (as shown in the figure on the left), as well as the type of alarm you hear at the end of your nap (I prefer the Tibetan Bowl, as you can see in the figure on the right). You can also choose any of six background soundtracks that have names such as Cranial Nirvana, Ocean, Sunrise, and Water Drop. Of course, you can determine how long you want to nap, as long as it's between 10 and 90 minutes.

Finally, Pzizz Relax uses a structured random algorithm with more than 100 billion voice/command/music/sound combinations, so you're assured of a different soundtrack each and every time you use it.

I love Pzizz Relax; but I have to admit that when I first heard about it I was skeptical. I've learned, though, that there's actually some science behind it, and several studies have determined that afternoon naps are indeed good for you. For example, a NASA study published in 1999 states that napping is one of the measures that can prevent fatigue and lack of focus and concluded that "an afternoon nap increases productivity by 35% and decision-making ability by up to 50%."

I don't understand how or why it works, but when I use Pzizz on my iPhone or my Mac to take a 15- or 20-minute power nap in the afternoon, I feel both energized and more relaxed the rest of the day. That's not a bad deal for three bucks.

Best features

The Pzizz applications for the Mac and Windows have a few features not found in the iPhone app, but they also cost $40 or more. There also used to be a stand-alone Pzizz hardware unit, now discontinued, which sold for about $150. The Pzizz Relax iPhone app delivers almost all the benefits of those products at a fraction of the price.

Worst features

One thing in Pzizz Relax is the same for every nap and that's the dude's voice. Although his voice is soothing and mellifluous, I'd love the option of other, preferably female, voices.

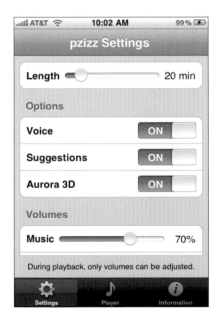
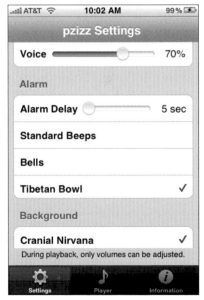

reQall
Free

reQall is a free app that helps you remember all the important things in your life. Or, as its App Store Application Description so aptly puts it, "reQall is a voice-enabled memory aid that seamlessly integrates your iPhone, e-mail, text messaging, and instant messaging into a powerful organizer, reminder system, and productivity assistant." Whew. I couldn't have said it better myself, which is why I quoted the App Store description.

I know what you're thinking: "Another app that claims it'll help me organize my life. Yawn." But reQall is smart and different from most organizer apps.

For one thing, although you can add items by typing them into the reQall app, you can also add them by voice, which is what I prefer. I tap the big blue + (plus sign) button that's in the upper-right corner of every reQall screen and say, for example, "Buy Lisa some flowers tonight."

Then the real magic begins. reQall first translates my words into text and then it does several cool things:

1. Because the first word is "buy," reQall puts this item on my reQall shopping list, as shown in the figure on the left.

2. Because the message also includes the word "tonight," reQall also puts this item on my to-do list for today.

3. Because I have set up reQall to e-mail me a copy of every reminder, a few minutes later I receive an e-mail message that reads, "buy Lisa some flowers tonight." The e-mail also includes the audio recording just in case the speech-to-text translation didn't come out right.

Usually, the voice recordings are spot on. In fact, one of the things I like best about reQall is that it translates what I say into text with close to 100% accuracy.

reQall also understands other words, such as *ask, tell, remind, meet, meeting, today, tomorrow, yesterday,* the days of the week, dates, and times (*11:00 a.m.,* for example). reQall can even create a recurring event if you start your recording with the words "each" or "every."

Furthermore, e-mail is only one of the options for receiving reminders. You can also have reminders sent via SMS text message, instant message, or push notification on your iPhone.

reQall enables you to share reminders with others and understands names when you speak them. So I can say something like, "Ask Lisa to check on our book order at Amazon.com." Because Lisa and her e-mail address are in my reQall contacts list, she receives an e-mail with the message and voice recording.

The icons you see along the bottom of the screen in the figure on the left represent different ways of organizing your reminder items. Jogger displays the Memory Jogger screen, a continuously updated summary of important items or items reQall thinks you may have forgotten. The Time screen displays items due today, soon (within seven days), later (beyond soon), and those items that are overdue. The Things screen contains to-do items, shopping list items, and notes. And the People screen shows people in your contacts and items you've shared with them. If you tap the little green check mark just above the People icon, you see a list of all recent reQall items, as shown in the figure on the right.

I have more to say about reQall, but my editor tells me I'm almost out of space. In closing, let me say everything I've described thus far is free, but for $2.99 per month or $24.99 per year, you can buy reQall Pro, which provides additional features such as reminders by SMS message and the capability to add items via e-mail. Visit www.reqall.com/about/compare_pro_standard for details.

Best features

It's free and does all the things I described above quite well.

Worst features

Occasionally voice-to-text translations take 30 minutes or more.

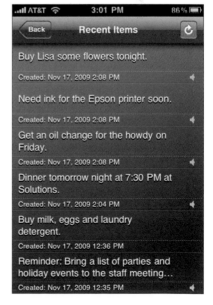

Instapaper Free
Free

Have you ever happened upon a Web page with a long and interesting story you really want to read but don't have the time? Or have you wished you could somehow stick the story in your pocket and read it during the train ride home, on the airplane, or at some other down time? If that has ever happened to you, you're going to love Instapaper Free, an app that lets you save Web pages so you can read them later with or without an Internet connection.

There's also Instapaper Pro ($4.99), which includes additional features such as folders, tilt-to-scroll, subscriptions, and more.

iTranslate
Free

It's true that you can use Safari to visit the free Google Translate Web service (http://translate.google.com/#), which can translate words, Web pages, and documents to and from more than 50 languages. For words and sentences (but not Web pages or documents) the free iTranslate app is easier to use, has smart auto correction and auto capitalization for better translation quality, and is prettier. It also auto-detects the language you're typing, remembers the last languages you used, and offers a choice of font sizes. You may prefer iTranslate Plus, which costs $1.99 and includes landscape mode support and a favorites list.

Pastie
$2.99 US

Pastie is a handy little app that lets you save commonly used expressions and messages — called "pasties" — for use in e-mail or SMS messages. You can also copy pasties to the clipboard to use in any iPhone app that supports copy and paste. You can even associate a pastie with a specific contact so you could, for example, send your wife an e-mail message that says, "I'm on my way. . . need anything at the store?" with one tap.

If you're not sure you'll like this app, try Pastie Lite, which is free but limits you to three pasties and two favorites.

ProPrompter
$9.99 US

If you speak in front of an audience or video camera, you'll love ProPrompter. Made by professional Teleprompter manufacturer Bodelin Technologies, ProPrompter turns your iPhone into a smooth-scrolling, professional quality Teleprompter. You can load scripts by e-mail, by using copy and paste, or via the free ProPrompter Producer Web site. The app provides complete control over fonts, font sizes, background colors, mirroring (for camera-top use like a real Teleprompter), cue points for fast access to specific parts of your speech, and on-the-fly scroll speed adjustment.

If you need a Teleprompter, ProPrompter does an excellent job and is a steal at just $9.99.

Use Your Handwriting
Free

Yes, Use Your Handwriting is yet another to-do list organizer/reminder type app. But this one has a unique twist: You can't type notes or even speak them. Instead, as the app's name implies, when you use Use Your Handwriting, you write your notes by hand. You actually write with your finger, not your hand, but you get the picture. You'll love the way the screen scrolls to let you write whole sentences.

If you hate typing on your iPhone's cramped keyboard or just have really nice handwriting (fingerwriting?), Use Your Handwriting may be the best choice for your list-making and reminder needs.

12 Reference

Art Envi Deluxe
$3.99 US

Having Art Envi Deluxe is like having the history of art in pictures and words on your iPhone. The app includes works by hundreds of artists, which are organized alphabetically by artist and also by periods that include Byzantine, Gothic, Baroque, Renaissance, Impressionism, and Modern. The app also offers sections on ancient art and Asian art.

Regardless of how you choose to explore the art — alphabetically or by period — you can find a dozen or more works by each artist arranged in a *Web Show.* In the figure on the left, I'm watching a Web Show about Rembrandt.

Art Envi Deluxe offers myriad options for viewing Web Shows. You can choose your favorite transition or allow the app to select an appropriate one. You can turn on the Ken Burns effect to provide the illusion of motion. You can view thumbnails of all the artwork in a show and tap individual pictures to see them. You can speed up, slow down, stop, or reverse the show at any time, and you can enlarge, shrink, or rotate any picture. You can turn captions on or off or display them briefly when a picture first appears. You can add music from your iTunes music library to any show, or you can delete any image and never see it again.

That's not all, though. You can also save any image from the app to your iPhone's Camera Roll or set any image as your wallpaper background. Another option lets you link from any image to the Web site from which it originated so that you can read additional facts and see other images. Of course, Art Envi Deluxe also includes detailed information about each artist, as shown in the figure on the right. For what it's worth, the text you see in the figure is merely the first of 29 pages of information about Rembrandt.

I'd be remiss if I didn't mention that there's also a non-deluxe version of this app, called Art Envi, that's only 99¢. At only $3.99 for the Deluxe version, however, you get nearly 100 more artists, more artwork by many of the artists, the capability to save images, and a faster display.

If art isn't your thing, there are dozens of other Envi apps: Architect Envi, Astronaut Envi, Amusement Park Envi, Antique Car Envi, Aston Martin Envi, Ferrari Envi, Ballpark Envi, Cat Envi, Comic Envi, Dog Envi, and at least one hundred other Envi apps. You can also get a free Envi Sampler that's a great way to find out if you enjoy the Envi experience enough to pay for one of the Envi apps.

Best features

Art Envi Deluxe is beautiful, flexible, scholarly, and fun. If you like to look at art or learn about it, you'll find an ample supply of artwork and information in Art Envi Deluxe.

Worst features

Because all the images are pulled from Web sites, the app is more or less useless if you don't have Internet access. Some pictures load slowly or don't load at all, depending upon Web traffic and the originating site's status, although this shortcoming isn't the fault of Art Envi Deluxe.

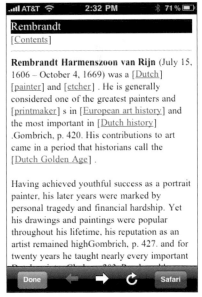

Google Mobile App
Free

According to its App Store description, "Google Mobile App is the fastest, easiest way to search Google." I'm usually not much for hyperbole, but I think the App Store's description is an understatement.

Here's why: I have big, fat fingers. I type at least 60 words per minute on the Microsoft Ergonomic Keyboard 4000 on my desk, but on an iPhone, I'm lucky to type six words per minute. An app that helps me get things done and saves me keystrokes — as Google Mobile App does — is a winner in my book (and, as it turns out, in *this* book).

Just launch Google Mobile App and hold your iPhone next to your ear. When you hear the tone, say what you want to search for. Really. You don't have to tap any buttons or do anything else. The app is super smart and uses your iPhone's proximity sensor to determine when it's next to your face. It then uses your iPhone microphone to determine when you're speaking, what you said, and when you're finished. Finally, it translates your speech into a Google search query and performs the search.

You can be extremely specific. For example, I told the app I wanted to see "pictures of the University of Texas tower at night," and that's exactly what Google Mobile App found for me, as you can see in the figure on the left.

Google Mobile App's voice recognition engine is extremely good. I said such things as "names of the members of Spinal Tap," "shepherd's pie recipe," "price of a 30-inch Apple Cinema Display," and "James Bond Aston Martin," and Google Mobile App translated every word correctly.

But wait! There's more! Even if you prefer typing to talking, are in a noisy location, lost your voice, or have a mouth numbed by Novocain, Google Mobile App is *still* the fastest and easiest way to search. In fact, when you type your query rather than speaking it, Google Mobile offers suggestions as you type, as shown in the figure on the right. For that picture I typed the word *auto,* and Google suggested Rational Automotive (a nearby auto repair shop that happened to be in my Address Book), a search for *auto* near my location, *autotrader, autozone,* and so on.

Did I mention that Google Mobile App is available in English, Chinese, Danish, Dutch, Finnish, French, German, Italian, Japanese, and at least half a dozen other languages? No? Well, it is.

And one last thing . . . an apps button at the bottom of the screen offers one-tap access to most Google apps and services including Gmail, Calendar, Talk, Docs, Tasks, Reader, GOOG-411, News, Notebook, Photos, Translate, Maps, and YouTube.

This is one of the coolest apps of all time. Its voice recognition prowess is as good as or better than any other speech-to-text application I know of, and I'm not comparing it only to iPhone apps, either. Google Mobile App does a better job recognizing speech than many Mac and PC programs — even some that require extensive user training. You can't beat the price, either; the app is free!

Best features

What's best about Google Mobile App? It's free; it understands pretty much anything you say; it translates your words into text with uncanny accuracy; and then it searches the Web for your query without any further intervention — not even a single tap — on your part. So everything about it is great except. . . .

Worst features

. . . the history feature remembers only your six most recent queries. For an app that's extremely excellent in every other respect, this limitation seems kind of lame.

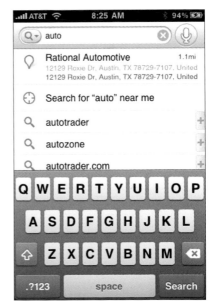

Oxford Deluxe — ODE & OTE with Audio

$54.99 US

The Oxford Deluxe app weighs in at more than 300 megabytes and includes the full text of the *Oxford Dictionary of English* (ODE), Second Edition, and the *Oxford Thesaurus of English* (OTE), Second Edition. The app also has high-quality audio recordings with more than 55,000 pronunciations. According to the publisher, it's the largest Oxford English reference available on any mobile platform.

I know you're probably thinking that $54.99 is a lot to pay for a dictionary and thesaurus, and you're right. But consider this: The hardcover second editions of the ODE and OTE have more than 3,000 pages; weigh 12 pounds; and have a combined cost of more than $100. Of course, because the ODE and OTE are actual *books* (what a concept!), they don't come with *any* audio recordings or fit in your pants pocket with room to spare for your wallet.

Not all dictionaries and thesauri are created equal. You can find plenty of decent dictionary apps, and some of them (including the Dictionary.com Dictionary & Thesaurus app described later in this chapter) are even free. If price is your only criteria for judging a dictionary, one of the free apps is probably good enough for you. If you are more concerned with accuracy and completeness, desire a superb user interface with unique and helpful features, and are willing to pay for a quality product, the Oxford Deluxe app is absolutely worth every penny.

As a writer, I have found the Oxford Deluxe app has many features that appeal to me. For example, I can use a question mark as a wild card search character if I'm not sure of a word's spelling, as shown in the picture on the left. Not all dictionary apps let me use wild card characters. In addition, I don't know of any other dictionary at any price that includes audio pronunciations, much less really good ones.

You can tap on almost any word in any definition in the dictionary or any synonym in the thesaurus to look up that word. I can bookmark pages to keep them handy while I work on a project. The app automatically keeps track of every word I look at and maintains them in separate histories for the dictionary and thesaurus. Plus, the history function doesn't appear to have an arbitrary limit; I used this app heavily for many days and every word I looked at is still available in the appropriate history tab. Finally, unlike most other reference apps, the Oxford Deluxe app doesn't require an Internet connection, so I can refer to it in places where many other reference apps would fail.

In addition to more than 300,000 words, phrases, definitions, and biographical references, the Oxford Deluxe app includes more than a dozen useful appendices, such as Countries of the World; States of the USA; Prime Ministers and Presidents; Kings and Queens; Weights, Measures, and Notation; Chemical Elements; Proofreading Marks; and Guide to Good English.

Although there are many things I like about the Oxford Deluxe app, there are a couple things that I don't much care for. I understand that Oxford is in England and this is an *English* dictionary in the strictest sense of the word, but I wish the app didn't use British spellings such as *defence* instead of *defense* and *colour* instead of *color* (although the pronunciation sounds okay to my American ear). Take a peek at the figure on the right to see what the app returned when I looked up *color.*

The other thing that bothers me is that words in the thesaurus don't include audio pronunciations even if the dictionary includes a pronunciation for the same word. That's just lazy.

Best features

The Oxford Deluxe app is comprehensive, authoritative, and easy to use; it doesn't require Internet access; and it includes audio pronunciations.

Worst features

British spellings take precedence.

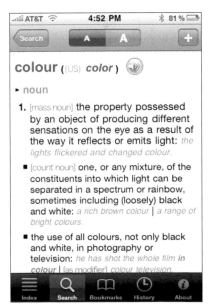

Wikipanion/Wikipanion Plus
Free/$4.99 US

Wikipanion and Wikipanion Plus are apps that make it easier to search and use Wikipedia. If you're not familiar with Wikipedia, it's the huge, crowd-sourced (meaning anyone can edit any article), free, online encyclopedia that includes more than three million articles (www. wikipedia.org). Wikipedia is not the last word on any topic, given the fact that anyone can edit articles. However, Wikipedia contributors are good about self-policing, so inaccuracies, slanted reporting, or worse generally don't last long before a conscientious user replaces the entry.

You can use Wikipedia with your iPhone's Safari Web browser. In fact, you should give that a try right now. Go ahead, I'll wait. . .

Now you know what Wikipedia looks like in Safari. Even though what you used was the special mobile version of Wikipedia that only appears if you reach the site using your iPhone (or other Web-enabled device), it's not exactly optimized for convenience, which is where the Wikipanion apps shine.

Both Wikipanion and Wikipanion Plus are crammed full of features that make it faster and easier for you to find what you need in Wikipedia. For example, one feature is smart text completion, which offers you suggested entries based on what you type. For example, when I type **Led Z** in the search field, the list of possible matches includes *Led Zeppelin, Led Zeppelin concerts, Led Zeppelin bootleg recordings, Led Zeppelin IV,* and so on. I tap the first entry, *Led Zeppelin,* and the resulting page is shown in the figure on the left.

Another advantage of using Wikipanion is that most lengthy entries include a table of contents, which lets you jump right to the information you need without making you wade through a bunch of information you don't care about. There's also in-page searching that enables you to find a word or phrase and jump right to it.

One of my favorite features is that links to other items related in some way to the article you're reading are only a tap away, as shown in the figure on the right. I find the links invaluable for brainstorming and discovering useful information I might never have thought of.

Other helpful features found in both Wikipanion and Wikipanion Plus include

- ✔ Bookmarks that can remember both the entries you view, as well as the specific sections of the entries
- ✔ History entries for as many as 100 items
- ✔ Dual language searching

✔ Interactive font resizing

✔ Integrated Wiktionary (Wikipedia's free dictionary and thesaurus) lookups

✔ Integrated audio playback with support for the Ogg vorbis audio format used in some Wikipedia entries and Wiktionary pronunciations

✔ No advertising

In addition to all of the above, Wikipanion Plus has two other features that many users (myself included) think are worth $5. The first is a queue. When this feature is enabled, any links you tap go on the queue list instead of being opened immediately. I like the queue feature because I can finish reading the main article and view the related items later, which means I don't have to do a lot of flipping back and forth. The page saver feature in Wikipanion Plus is the one I find most appealing. With it I can manually or automatically save articles and links in my queue for offline reading. This rocks because, like many reference apps, Wikipanion and Wikipanion Plus are virtually worthless when you don't have an Internet connection.

Best features

Both versions of the app make it faster and easier to search for things in Wikipedia; the queue and page saver in Wikipanion Plus make using Wikipedia on the iPhone even better.

Worst features

You can't do searches with Wikipanion or Wikipanion Plus unless you have Internet access.

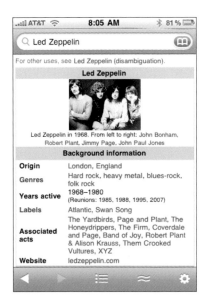

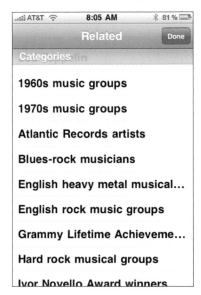

The World Factbook
$3.99 US

The World Factbook app is the definitive source of reliable information about the nations of the world. It contains up-to-date information about more than 250 countries and territories, and it has a fast and easy-to-use interface.

The app works almost exactly like Safari, with forward and back buttons, bookmarks, and a history feature. The information provided for each nation includes the flag, a map of the location, and nine categories of information: Introduction, Geography, People, Government, Economy, Communications, Transportation, Military, and Transnational Issues.

The Geography category provides information such as the country's general location, geographic coordinates, land mass and boundaries, climate, and terrain, as shown in the figure on the left. The Geography category also includes a substantial amount of information on international agreements the country has signed.

The People category describes the nation's population by size, age, growth, birth and death rates, life expectancy, ethnicity, religion, languages, and dozens of other facts about the nation's indigenous people.

In the Government category, you can find data about the country's type of government, its capital, administrative divisions, national holidays, legal system, age of suffrage, and a detailed description of the branches of its government, political parties and leaders, and its diplomatic representation to and from the U.S.

The Economy category begins with a few tightly written paragraphs about the nation's economic situation. That's followed by a mind-numbing list of statistics and figures that includes several measures of Gross Domestic Product (GDP), labor force makeup and unemployment rate, information about income and investments, public debt, annual national budget, lending and discount rates, major industries, agricultural products, energy, imports and exports, and tons of additional economic data.

The Communications category covers infrastructure, the number of land and mobile cellular telephone lines in use, description of the telephone system, plus detailed information about radio and television stations, Internet hosts, and Internet users.

The Transportation category includes information on airports and their runway lengths, as well as key data for pipelines, heliports, railways, roads, ports, and terminals.

The Military category discusses (what else?) the nation's military — its branches, service age, service obligation, manpower available for and fit for military service, and military expenditures.

Finally, the Transnational Issues category is where you find information about disputes the nation is currently involved in, its refugees and internally displaced persons, illicit drug activity, and other bits of information that don't fit cleanly into any of the other categories.

Unlike some reference apps, The World Factbook does not require Internet access, but it only consumes about 10MB of space on your iPhone. Furthermore, the publisher regularly provides free updates to the data.

If you're involved in any kind of international business or product marketing, plan to travel abroad, are a writer of fiction or non-fiction books with an international orientation, or are just a person who likes to have facts at your fingertips, The World Factbook is just the ticket.

Best features
The World Factbook contains an incredible amount of detailed information, uses a tiny fraction of your iPhone's storage capacity, doesn't require Internet access, and is fast and easy to use.

Worst features
The only graphics included are the nation's flag and a map. More images are the only thing I can think of that would make this app better than it already is.

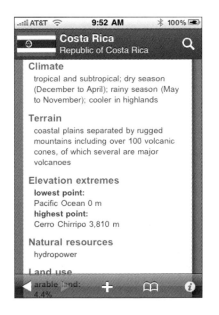
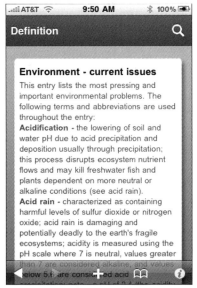

Dial Zero
Free

Wouldn't it be nice to call a company's customer service hot line and know exactly which keys to press to skip immediately to a live person? If you think so, you're going to love the free Dial Zero app, which lets you skip all those annoying recorded voice prompts and jump straight to a living being without delay. With listings for more than 600 companies and lots of comments by users, you not only can skip the boring blather, but you may even pick up a tip or two for successfully dealing with the company's service personnel.

Dictionary.com Dictionary & Thesaurus
Free

This app is probably the best of the free dictionary and thesaurus apps currently available. It includes world-class reference content from Dictionary.com and Thesaurus.com with more than 275,000 definitions and 80,000 synonyms, and it even has audio pronunciations. Furthermore, although the audio, Word of the Day, and similarly spelled words features do require Internet access, the dictionary and thesaurus don't. That means you can have most of the app's functionality even when you don't have a network connection.

Dictionary.com Dictionary & Thesaurus is not as comprehensive as the Oxford Deluxe app, but it's still a terrific resource. And you sure can't complain about the price since it's free.

The Elements of Style By William Strunk, Jr.
$0.99 US

I think *The Elements of Style* — written in 1918 by William Strunk Jr. and E.B. White — is the best style guide ever for anyone who wants to learn to write proper American English. I keep a copy of the book within arm's reach at all times, and I read it cover to cover (it's fewer than 100 pages) at least once each year. With simple yet practical advice such as "omit needless words" and "use the active voice," and clear, concise examples, you should absolutely keep this app (or paperback) handy if anything you write will be read by others.

MathRef
$0.99 US

If you're into math and would like a handy pocket reference with more than 1,000 formulas, figures, tips, and examples of equations and concepts, MathRef may be the best 99¢ you ever spend. With categories for algebra, geometry, trigonometry, linear algebra, series and sequences, derivatives, integration, vector calculus, differential equations, prime numbers, and more, it packs a lot of helpful info in an inexpensive and easy-to-use app.

Check the App Store for these categories that are currently listed as "coming soon": basic chemistry, statistics, accounting and financial, real estate, equation editor, and quadratic equation solver.

Your Rights
Free

Do you know your rights in the event government agents detain or question you? If you don't but would like to, this free app is a winner. It is based on information provided by the American Civil Liberties Union and, although the app isn't a substitute for good legal counsel, it is an excellent overview of your rights if you are stopped, questioned, arrested, or searched by a law enforcement officer. Because anything you say to an officer can and will be used against you, wouldn't you feel a whole lot better knowing exactly what your rights are in such situations?

13 Social Networking

AppConnect
Free

AppConnect helps you find new apps and recommendations of cool apps from other app lovers. But that's not all . . . it also shows you apps that are new or popular at the App Store. Plus, you can use it to meet other app lovers and see what they recommend. My absolute favorite feature is that I can receive a notification when the price of a specific app is lowered. Best of all, you get all this and more absolutely free!

I'd be remiss if I didn't at least mention that plenty of free apps are available to help you find cool new iPhone apps, such as AppMiner, PandoraBox, BargainBin, AppSniper, and App Gems. There is also at least one Web site, Appolicious.com, which attempts to integrate social networking with recommendations for iPhone apps. But, in my humble opinion, the AppConnect iPhone app is the best mash up of iPhone app recommendations and social networking.

Even if you hate social networking or don't have any friends, AppConnect is still great for finding cool iPhone apps. For example, the figure on the left shows the listing of apps on sale and those that are currently free. If you tap the Paid button near the top of the screen, you see apps that have reduced prices. If you tap the AppPoint button, you see apps that are on sale — but in this case they're ranked by AppConnect user votes.

On the same screen you can also check out new apps and apps that are hot (bestsellers). They're listed by the same criteria as the apps on sale, namely Free, Paid, and AppPoint. All this adds up to a lot of different ways to discover new, popular, recommended, or discounted apps. Then, when you find an app that interests you, you can read more about it in AppConnect, or you can tap a button to buy it or read more about it in the App Store.

On the social side of things, you can read reviews posted by other AppConnect users. When you find users you feel share your taste in apps, ask those people to be your friends. After they accept, you'll see an alert any time they post a new app review.

Another thing I like is AppConnect's capability to track prices on apps I'm willing to buy if the price is reduced, such as Madden NFL 10 and Rock Band. You can see the Tracking indicator in the figure on the right. If any of the ten apps I'm tracking goes on sale, I see an alert when I launch AppConnect.

Best features

The best thing about AppConnect is that it offers so many ways to discover new apps. You can also see what other users recommend, and you can recommend your favorite apps to other users. Finally, AppConnect notifies you when apps you specify go on sale.

Worst features

I sometimes forget to check AppConnect for days on end, so I wish it had push notification that would alert me of price reductions as soon as they occur.

BeeJiveIM with Push
$9.99 US

If you like to keep in touch with your friends via instant messaging (IM), and if you use more than one of the popular instant messaging services — AIM, MobileMe, MSN/Windows Live, Yahoo!, GoogleTalk, Facebook, My Space, ICQ, and Jabber — you are going to love BeeJiveIM.

An app that lets you use nine different IM services and works beautifully regardless of which network your iPhone is using — 3G, EDGE, or WiFi — is pretty cool. The capability to use any or all of the services at the same time, as shown in the figure on the left, makes BeeJiveIM even cooler. You can see that I'm available on all five of the IM services I use (from left to right after the word "Online"): MobileMe/AIM, Jabber, MySpace, Yahoo!, and Facebook.

Now check out how my Available message says, "Talk to me. . ." for MobileMe, AIM, Jabber, and MySpace. That's because I'm lazy. If I were more ambitious, I could have set a different message for each service, or set any or all of them to indicate that I was Away, Busy, or Invisible.

But wait; there's more! Not only can you chat via nine different IM services at once, you can log in using multiple accounts on any or all of the services. BeeJiveIM can monitor dozens of accounts on up to nine different instant message services at one time.

As long as you have an account with either AIM or Yahoo!, you can send messages to any SMS-equipped cell phone without paying a single penny to your wireless provider (AT&T in the U.S.). The recipients may have to pay the normal cost of SMS messages, but they'd have to pay that even if you sent your text messages via AT&T. BeeJiveIM integrates with your iPhone address book, so you can choose text message recipients the same way you would if you used the bundled Messages app (with its associated per-message charges from AT&T).

The *Push* in the app's name means you can close the app and still receive alert notifications when messages arrive. Better still, you can choose how you want to be notified — by an on-screen alert or by e-mail.

Another cool feature is that BeeJiveIM can send and receive pictures and voice notes as long as the IM service you're using supports it, as most of them do.

Last, but definitely not least, BeeJiveIM has the longest list of available options I've ever seen in a single iPhone app, including groups, meta chat, number of messages to preview in lists, auto-correct, auto-capitalization, and emoticon support.

Oh, there is one more thing: If you use only one or two instant message services, you probably don't need to spend ten bucks on BeeJiveIM. Some really nice free clients are available for each of the individual services, some of which are featured later in this chapter. But if you have friends on all the available services, as shown in the figure on the right below, it's just the ticket.

Best features

This app costs $9.99, but the capability to send and receive SMS text messages at no additional cost could be worth a lot more than that to you. Plus BeeJiveIM's capability to access up to nine instant message services at once is pretty sweet, as are the push notifications for incoming messages. If free SMS text messages appeal to you, and you'd like to use the same app for IMs and free SMS messaging, you may prefer BeeJiveIM to a stand-alone free app such as textPlus, which is described later in this chapter. Finally, if you prefer e-mail notifications to on-screen notifications, BeeJiveIM can handle that, too.

Worst features

BeeJiveIM suffers from occasional crashes and push notification delays. Fortunately, I experience both issues infrequently and, as far as I can tell, only a few other users have reported them.

Skype
Free

Skype is a service that offers free voice calls and text messages to tens of millions of Skype users. There's no charge for your Skype account or for the Skype software, which is available for the iPhone and iPod touch as well as Mac OS X, Windows, Linux, Windows Mobile, Nokia N800/810, and even the Sony PSP.

After you've set up your free account, you can make free Skype-to-Skype voice calls to any other Skype user anywhere on earth for free. You can also chat with other Skype users for free.

What do you do if your friends don't have Skype? Well, they *could* download and install Skype on their Macs, PCs, iPhones, or whatever, and sign up for a free account. If that's not going to happen for some reason, Skype also lets you make calls to landlines and mobile phones for low prices.

For example, you can currently sign up for unlimited calls to U.S. and Canadian landlines and mobile phones for €2.24 a month (around $3.20 US at press time). Or you can get unlimited calls to landlines (and some mobiles) in more than 40 countries (as shown in the figure on the left) for €8.95 (less than $15 US at press time). Better still, no long-term contract is required. If you don't want to take advantage of an unlimited calling plan, you can pay as you go, with á la carte pricing starting at less than 5¢ per minute. For example, when our son spent the summer in Israel, we called him via Skype (as shown in the figure on the right) and paid approximately 3¢ per minute instead of the 21¢ per minute or more it would have cost via AT&T.

For a few dollars a month you can even get an inbound Skype phone number (known as a SkypeIn number), so anyone can call you on Skype from any landline or mobile phone anywhere in the world. Other low-cost Skype options include voicemail, SMS messaging, call forwarding, and caller ID.

I use SkypeIn for my consulting business and pay about $70 per year for all the aforementioned services, unlimited calling to U.S. and Canadian landlines and mobile phones, and discounted rates for calls to other countries. My technicians and I can check for voicemail using the Skype iPhone app and return calls to clients anywhere in the world for much less than it would cost to dial via AT&T.

There is one notable downside to Skype: At present you can only make and receive calls via Wi-Fi. Although most of the other services, including voicemail and chat, work fine over EDGE or 3G, voice calling over the cellular networks is currently prohibited. That's the bad news. The good news is that on October 6, 2009 AT&T announced it will soon take the steps necessary to enable VoIP (Voice over Internet Protocol) apps — such as Skype — on the iPhone, over the 3G network. Nobody knows exactly when this will happen, and still no word as this book goes to press. Stay tuned.

Best features

Skype has tons of great features. At the top of the list has to be that it gives you the capability to call millions of Skype users all over the world for free. The reduced rates for calls to landlines and mobile phones in other countries are pretty sweet, too, as is the reasonable cost for an inbound (SkypeIn) phone number with caller ID, voicemail, and call forwarding.

Worst features

Voice calls are currently restricted to Wi-Fi networks and are sometimes less reliable than the same calls made over the AT&T mobile network.

textPlus
Free

Under ordinary circumstances, you use the Messages app that comes bundled with your iPhone to send and receive SMS text messages. The only problem is that only a limited number of text messages (or possibly none) are included in your iPhone data plan. My AT&T plan in the U.S., for example, includes only 200 SMS messages a month. Your mileage may vary.

Well, I happen to have a couple of teen kids who each can easily send more than 200 SMS messages *a day* on a slow day. SMS messages beyond the 200 per month that's part of our plan cost $0.20 each or $15 for 1,500 a month. Other options include unlimited SMS messages for $20 a month per person and unlimited SMS messages for a family for $30.

The bottom line is that SMS messages can get real expensive real fast. And that's what makes the textPlus app a winner. With textPlus, you can send and receive unlimited SMS text messages at absolutely no cost to you. Recipients pay for their text messages as usual unless they also use textPlus, in which case their SMS messages are also completely free.

Like the Messages app, textPlus has push notification, so it can alert you of incoming messages even if textPlus isn't running. Unlike the Messages app, though, textPlus censors your messages, stripping out most four-letter words and replacing them with asterisks. textPlus outperforms other free SMS apps, however, and has a better user interface, so I still recommend it — in spite of the censorship.

textPlus works pretty much the same way the bundled Messages app works with a couple of notable exceptions. The first difference, which I think is the best, is that you can initiate group conversations with multiple recipients. It's great that all of the participants in a conversation can see and respond to every subsequent message from every participant, as shown in the figure on the left.

Another difference is that textPlus is advertiser-supported, so there are small ads on most of its screens, like the one for Ps2 Repairs that you can see near the bottom of the figure on the left.

The Messages app can send SMS messages to and receive SMS messages from any cellular network provider, but textPlus only works with some of the majors, including AT&T, Verizon, Sprint, T-Mobile, Alltel, US Cellular, Virgin Mobile, Nextel, Boost, Cellular One, Dobson, Cellular South, and CellCom. At this time, other carriers — including

MetroPCS and Cricket — are not supported by textPlus, which means you can't use the app to exchange SMS messages with anyone who gets service from one of the unsupported carriers. Because you probably don't know which carrier your friends use, this could be a problem for you.

Finally, even though your real name shows up as part of your message, the message appears to be coming from a series of random numbers instead of your name. The figure on the right shows how a message I sent to my wife looked in the Messages app on her iPhone. Put another way, what she saw was (606) 110-02; what she should have seen in that space was my name.

Best features

The best thing about textPlus is that it provides you with unlimited free SMS text messages, but the group conversations and push notifications are pretty nice, too.

Worst features

A couple of messages I sent never got to their recipient(s). Perhaps they were users of an unsupported service, though I never received any feedback that they were (or that the recipients never received my messages). However, I didn't find that problem nearly as vexing as the fact that this app censors your words.

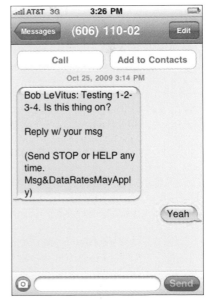

Tweetie 2
$2.99 US

My name is Bob, and I am a Twitterholic. I follow the tweets of people I know, of people I like, and of people who interest me. I post my own tweets whenever I have something to say.

If you didn't understand the previous paragraph, you must not be a Twitter fan. Twitter, for those of you who have lived in a cave for the past few years, is a so-called *micro-blogging* service. It allows users to post short messages called *tweets*. The twist is that a tweet has to be 140 characters or fewer, which, thankfully, forces most users to omit needless words.

You can follow people and read their tweets with any Web browser at Twitter.com (if you care to check out my tweets, my username is "LeVitus"). But, as every Twitter aficionado knows, it's easier and more fun to use Twitter with one of the specialized apps known as Twitter clients.

If you search the iTunes Store for Twitter clients, you'll find dozens. Many are free and most work just fine. After testing more than a dozen popular Twitter clients, Tweetie 2 has become my favorite.

I'll tell you about my favorite free Twitter client later in this chapter.

First and foremost, Tweetie 2's user interface is beautiful, elegant, easy to comprehend, and easy to use. It is designed in such a way that any feature I need is just one or two taps away. For example, while I'm typing a tweet, I can tap the little button that shows a triangle and number (as shown in the figure on the left) to reveal additional options.

In the figure, the number *4* on the button indicates that I have used 136 characters in my tweet and have 4 characters left before I reach the 140-character limit.

When I tap the button, the keyboard retracts and the six buttons shown at the bottom of the figure on the left replace it. Suffice it to say that those buttons — Camera, Photo Library, Geotag, Usernames, Hashtags, and Shrink URLs — represent useful features for composing tweets.

Another thing that makes Tweetie 2 superior to many other Twitter clients is that it works even if you don't have a network connection. So, for example, if you're on an airplane you can read tweets, reply to tweets, compose new tweets, follow or unfollow other users, and even specify your favorite tweets. As soon as you have a network connection, everything is synced and your pending tweets are sent and received automatically.

Unlike some other Twitter clients, Tweetie 2 lets you save as many draft tweets as you like and manages them with aplomb. If you perform many searches (as I do), Tweetie 2 lets you save them for reuse and even syncs them with the Tweetie 2 client for the Mac (sorry, Windows users).

Another neat feature is the map view, which uses your iPhone's GPS capabilities to display on a map tweets from nearby Twitter users.

Best features

I can't think of anything about Tweetie 2 that I don't like. I love the clean user interface (see the figure on the right) and how easy it is to access the features I use most. I also love the offline mode, which lets me read and write tweets even at 35,000 feet with no network access.

Worst features

I don't really think there is a worst feature, so I'm going to gripe about a feature I'd like to see in a future version of Tweetie 2 — push notification for specific messages. For example, if someone sent a message to my user name (@LeVitus) or replied to a tweet I had posted, I'd love to have my iPhone alert me immediately. I don't know of any other Twitter clients that have this feature, so maybe it's technically impossible, but it sure would be nice.

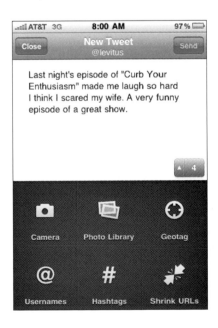

AIM
Free/$2.99 US

AIM is the official client app for the AOL Instant Messenger (AIM) service. If you don't want to shell out $2.99, you can choose an ad-supported free version.

Aside from the ads in the free version, the two versions are the same. With either version you can post photos, send and receive free SMS text messages, find out if your buddies are nearby, and chat with anyone on the AIM network worldwide (which includes AOL, AIM, ICQ, .Mac, and MobileMe users).

If you don't use other instant messaging services (such as MSN/Windows Live, Yahoo!, GoogleTalk, Facebook, My Space, or Jabber), the AIM app may be the only IM client you ever need.

Facebook
Free

If you visit Facebook (www.facebook.com) using your iPhone's Safari Web browser, I've got a treat for you. The free Facebook app does everything you can do in a Web browser but is designed specifically for your iPhone's 3.5-inch touch screen. It also includes iPhone-specific features, such as displaying on the app's icon the number of notifications you have waiting. The Facebook app has comprehensive photo-management tools so you can add and delete albums and photos, as well as upload photos and videos (iPhone 3GS only).

Download this free app and I virtually guarantee you'll never again use Safari on your iPhone to visit Facebook.

MySpace Mobile
Free

If you visit MySpace (www.myspace.com) using your iPhone's Safari Web browser, I have a treat for you. Like the Facebook app I described in the preceding section, the MySpace Mobile app makes it easier to send and receive MySpace messages, see your friends' statuses, update your status, upload photos, post comments, and search for friends. Where Safari is difficult to use and requires a lot of precise tapping and zooming in and out, the MySpace Mobile app has a sleek user interface designed to make things easier to do on an iPhone.

If you use MySpace, even occasionally, you're going to love the free MySpace Mobile app.

Twitterific
Free/$3.99 US

Twitterific is another Twitter client app, and I must say that Twitterific is also an apt description of the app. (See the description of Tweetie 2 earlier in the chapter to find out more about Twitter.) In fact, if I wasn't so happy with Tweetie 2, I'd probably use Twitterific.

As with the AIM client app, there's an ad-supported free version of Twitterific, as well as an ad-free version that costs $3.99. Both versions are feature-rich, with unified timelines that include replies, direct messages, and favorites, plus filtering and customizable visual themes and layouts.

If you're not ready to spend money on a Twitter client, the free version of Twitterific is just the ticket.

Yelp
Free

Yelp (www.yelp.com) helps you find great places to eat, shop, and do much more in dozens of U.S. cities. The Yelp iPhone app does the same thing, and it also helps you find great restaurants, bars, and other businesses that are near your current location.

When you find a business that interests you, a single tap lets you see its location, get driving directions, dial its phone number, visit its Web site, or read reviews written by local Yelp users. And because it's an iPhone app, many reviews include pictures of the food or services.

My family has discovered a lot of great restaurants and stores with Yelp, and we wholeheartedly recommend this app.

14 Sports

ESPN ScoreCenter
Free (ad supported)

You know, ESPN has been kicking sports butt since it burst onto the scene as one of the first all-sports cable networks in 1979. Although I'll be the first to admit that I'm not the world's biggest sports nut — hey, I'm Dr. Mac, not Dr. J! — a lot of what I do enjoy seems to be involved with ESPN in one way or another. So, ESPN's iPhone app — ESPN ScoreCenter, a play on the network's signature TV show *SportsCenter* — had a high bar to meet when I checked it out. I'm here to tell you that it cleared that bar, and then some.

First and foremost, I love that I get some sports trivia and history when I first launch the app. On the loading screen right underneath the logo, you get two lines of information. And this isn't just stuff that's loaded into the app that you'll cycle through faster than you can say, "Pass the ball": At least some of it is current information that's coming off the company's servers. I know I'm an information junkie, but I just think it's cool when an iPhone app can keep me engaged while it's still loading!

After the app is loaded, you'll find a very comprehensive app for keeping up-to-date with all the scores for your favorite teams across the NFL, Major League Baseball (MLB), the NBA, the WNBA, NCAA football, basketball, baseball, lacrosse, volleyball, water polo, NASCAR, Formula 1, IndyCar, golf, tennis, soccer/football, and even cricket and rugby. That's just pretty much nuts! The company says on iTunes that "much more" is in store for the future, if you can believe that.

Check out the figure on the left. It's the results for week 12 of the 2009/2010 NFL season. The Dallas Cowboys and Oakland Raiders are in the big square at the top, and that's because I set the Cowboys as my favorite team. Scores are displayed for all three games that were played on Thanksgiving, and below that are the matchups coming later on Sunday of that week, including the team's win/loss record, the time the game will be played, and the team logos. If I tap any of those squares, I either get the results and stats for the game with another link to a game wrap-up if the game has been played, or I get season/preview stats with a link to a game preview for games that have yet to be played.

In the figure on the right, you see the results for the Stanford Cardinal women's basketball game against the Utah Utes. The score, top performers (some games have more information on this screen than others), and a link to the deeper Recap are all displayed.

I found the women's games to have fewer stats in the opening window. But if you click through to the ESPN Mobile Web Recap, you can find everything you might be looking for: stats, game summary, and recap. In fact, this is true for just about every kind of game, so don't be afraid to poke around in the app if there's something you're expecting to find that's not readily apparent.

You can set up pages for whatever sports interest you with favorite teams for each, and you can tie into myESPN for syncing up your ScoreCenter teams with your online myESPN account. Unlike a lot of apps from large media companies, however, you aren't required to have an account to get the most out of it.

Best features
This app has an awesome interface, is intuitive, and has comprehensive score coverage of just about everything. I've been seriously impressed by this app.

Worst features
I couldn't find a way to quickly get back to the top of long lists of scores. I should be able to double-tap the title bar on any individual page to jump back up to the top.

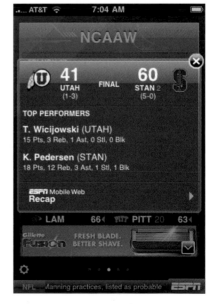

Fox Sports Mobile
Free (ad supported)

Fox Sports Mobile doesn't cover nearly as many different types of sports as ESPN ScoreCenter, but it offers deeper coverage of those sports that are there, including news, videos, stats, standings, and team information. This app offers a lot of stuff!

When you first launch the app, you get the Home screen. This is a general sporting information page with recent Fox Sports news stories and videos and a link to Scores.

 To get to specific sports (or a different sport if you're already in an individual sport), tap the Scores button on the Home screen, or tap the button in the top-right corner that is confusingly labeled with the current sport, but is really a link to the list of sports offered in the app.

If you tap the Scores tab, you are presented with a list of 14 different sports covered in the app as of this writing. These include the NFL, MLB, NASCAR, NCAA football, NCAA men's and women's basketball, the NBA, the NHL, soccer/football, golf, tennis, mixed martial arts, boxing, and the WNBA. Like I said, it's not as comprehensive a list as ESPN ScoreCenter, but it's still a lot of sports coverage.

Pick one and you get a new page dedicated to that sport, complete with a new set of dedicated tabs at the bottom of the screen (see the figure on the left) for News, Scores, Teams, Standings, and More.

 To get back to the home page with general sports articles and videos, tap the button in the top right of the screen and choose Home from the list of sports.

It's pretty obvious what News and Scores are, but tap through to the Teams tab, where you can find a list of all the teams in the sport or sporting league you're in — in this case, the NFL. Pick a team, say the Arizona Cardinals, and you're taken to a page dedicated to that team, with News, Schedule, Stats, and Roster subtabs at the top of the screen.

News offers what you'd expect, a list of recent news articles that pertain to the Cardinals, but we also get items like a cheat sheet that includes what is best described as handicapper advice, and several different kinds of reports, so dig around in the News subtab to see what you can discover. The other subtabs are self-explanatory.

If you go back to the main tabs for each sporting category, you can check out the Stats tab, which is a list of the top 12 performers in the various stats pertinent to the game. In the NBA, for instance, you can see some 14 different stats from assist/turnover ratio to turnovers per game. To choose a new stat, tap the button at the top of the screen, which you can see in the figure on the right, for a slot machine wheel with all 14 stats covered in this sport. Spin the wheel to the stat you want, tap Select, and you're taken to it.

Each of the sports covered offers different levels of coverage — mixed martial arts and boxing, for instance, only offered a News tab at the time of this writing — but this changes depending on what's going on in that individual sport at any given time. That's the beauty of a dynamic iPhone app that pulls a lot of its content from the Internet.

Best features

Fox Sports Mobile offers plenty of deep coverage on a variety of major sports.

Worst features

To get from sport to sport, you tap the button in the top-right corner (see either figure below), which is labeled with the sport you are currently in. That's unintuitive (and frankly silly), but it's a small nit-pick for an otherwise solid app. I should also mention that Fox Sports Mobile relies on simple lists for a lot of features, which is a bit plain to look at.

JIRBO Paper Football Signature Edition
$4.99 US

I remember spending a lot of time playing paper football in the lunch-room when I was a kid. I'd work on making the perfect paper football, which involves taking a half sheet of notebook paper and folding it in such a way that results in a thick triangle of tightly folded paper. I always wanted mine to have nice sharp corners, and of course you wanted to do it in such a way that it wouldn't come unfolded as you played. Ahh, the good ol' days, but who has time for such shenanigans today? Maybe kids today still play paper football, but with iPods and iPhones as ubiquitous today as Trapper notebooks were when I was a kid, I suspect there are fewer paper footballers today than at any time since the game was invented.

But I digress from my digression, which was to explain how the game is played. You and your opponent sit on opposite sides of a table, and you take turns flicking your paper football with the goal of getting it to stop with part of it hanging off the edge of the table without knocking it off. That's called a touchdown, and it's worth 6 points. After a touch-down you can try for an extra point by having your opponent make a goal with his fingers, while you try to knock the football through the air between his (or her!) fingers. If you do, that's an extra point.

Today we live in more digital times, and thanks to JIRBO, we can engage in a game of paper football without the risk of kicking our paper foot-ball onto the guy's desk three cubicles down or having to ask the head cheerleader if she wouldn't mind fetching your football out of her pud-ding. No, with JIRBO Paper Football Signature Edition, the only thing you risk is someone looking over your shoulder, calling you a dork, and then sitting down and asking if they can play the winner.

The object in this game is the same as the analog version: You want to flick your paper football across the table so that part of it is hanging over the edge. To do so, you start your sliding motion with your fingertip on the table, and then slide it toward the paper football. When your finger contacts the paper football, it moves. The faster you slide your finger, the farther the ball goes. Too soft, and it won't move much, whereas sliding it too hard sends the paper football over the edge of the table. The direc-tion of your slide and angle of incidence when it contacts the paper foot-ball determine the direction it slides across the table.

If you score a touchdown — see the figure on the left — the game enters Kick mode, where you can try and score an extra point, as you can see in the figure on the right. Direction and strength-of-contact with your slide really matter here.

You can play against the computer or in two-player mode with both players getting a side of the iPhone, just like in real life across a table. The game also tracks worldwide high scores from other players, where you can see some pretty outrageous scores.

If you're having trouble with your kicks, you can practice kicking in the Kick Mode tab, where you can kick again and again against an always-patient opponent who doesn't mind being your goal post until you're done practicing.

There's a free (ad supported) version of the game, too, where games are time-limited.

Best features

It's fun, and it will take you back to those days of playing paper football in the school cafeteria.

Worst features

Limited physics make such moves as the spinning football all but impossible, and don't get me started on how a paper football balances with 98% of it hanging over the edge!

MLB.com At Bat

$9.99 US during season
Free during off-season

I'm writing this after the World Series of 2009 is over, but MLB.com At Bat was a fantastic app during the 2009 season and post-season. Take a look at what you get for free during the off-season.

During the off-season, you get news, video, team information, and all the stats from the previous season, which is just perfect for you baseball junkies whiling away the hours until spring training arrives.

The News tab offers you a news feed of everything baseball-related in chronological order. Off-season trades, speculation, house cleaning and reorganizations, financial news: It's all there. The Videos tab is comprised of recent short clips as found on MLB.com, and the Teams tab is simply a way to get your news filtered by individual teams. You also find links to each team's Web site, which open in Safari. In the More tab, you find all those past-season stats, league standings, an FAQ for the app, and your settings.

But it's during the baseball season that MLB.com At Bat really shines, with live streaming video, real-time box scores, and game stats, as shown in the figure on the left, and much more.

For example, not only can you listen to radio broadcasts, but you often have a choice of the home or away team broadcast! That's way cool. If you have a favorite team, you can even have MLB.com At Bat always choose your team's audio feed.

My favorite feature, however, is that for games with video (usually two a day), you get to choose from different camera feeds. It's like being the director and calling your own shots! For most games, the feeds include Centerfield, Tight Centerfield, Blimp Cam, High Home Plate, Low First Base, Low Third Base, plus a Slow-Mo Replay view and Quad Mode, which divides the screen into quarters and shows you quarter-screen sized video feeds from four different cameras.

If it's baseball-related, it's in this app. There are stats galore, team standings, video highlights, text summaries (as shown in the figure on the right), and another of my favorites, the condensed game video that appears shortly after the end of many (if not most) games.

The video quality ranges from not bad to extremely pixilated and fuzzy. And although it's usually better over Wi-Fi than 3G, sometimes it's inexplicably worse over Wi-Fi. I have never really figured out why some video is better than other video. Sometimes 3G video looks pretty good; other times, it looks horrible. Video over Wi-Fi is no better (or worse).

Another thing I have to mention is that some postseason games were not available in At Bat 2009. On the other hand, the World Series *was* available, and being able to follow the game no matter where I happened to be was awesome.

Best features

At Bat is chock-full of features aimed squarely at baseball fans and at $9.99 for the entire 2009 season, it was a bargain.

Worst features

Video quality is unpredictable and some games are unavailable or blacked out in certain areas.

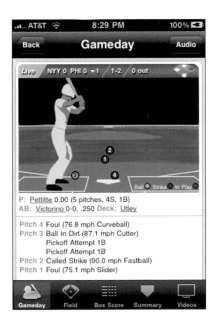
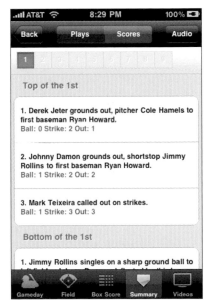

Sportacular Pro
$1.99 US

You know, I hear some people gamble on sporting events and games. I wouldn't know anything about that, but Sportacular Pro is a sporting scores app that also aims to please those who may be interested in that other aspect of sports. Don't get me wrong — this isn't some kind of betting app. Sportacular Pro lets you pick winners and see what other users have picked for that game, complete with a demographic breakdown across the U.S. In addition, the app gives you the current odds on a game.

First, take a look at the fundamentals of this app. You can get scores for the NFL, MLB, the NBA, the NHL, MLS, NCAA football, NCAA basketball (men and women), soccer/football, and golf (PGA, LPGA, PGA Championships, EURO PGA, and PGA Nationwide). Scores include both current game and past scores for leagues, and you can get upcoming schedules, as well. For instance, with the NFL, the game defaults to pulling up the current week (when in season), and you can tap through past weeks for past scores or future weeks for those schedules.

To change sports, tap the button at the top left of the screen with the sporting icon (like a football if you're in the NFL), and you get a list of all the offered sports. Tap a new sport, and you go to the Scores tab for that sport. It's on the Scores tab, by the way, where you can get odds for upcoming games. This isn't turned on by default, so you can either shake your iPhone when in this tab, or tap the button in the top right of the screen. If the game has already been played, you'll see the score, as you can see in the figure on the left. If the game is still to be played, you get the point spread, as well as the over/under (o/u) for the game, also in that figure. If betting isn't your thing, just leave this off and you won't be confronted by it.

Now, tap one of those games, and you get a little more information on the game, including the date and time (if it's yet to be played, the teams' win/loss records, their position in whatever league or subleague they're in, and the current betting line (regardless of whether the odds are turned on). You are also given the option of picking a winner, and after you make your pick, you see what other users have picked. Looking at an NBA game between the Celtics and the Heat, I just happened to go with other Sportacular users by (randomly) picking the Celtics, as you can see in the figure on the right. If I tap the View Map button, I get a regional breakdown of picks, where I can drill down further and get a breakdown by individual state. That's pretty cool, if you're into that sort of thing.

I can also chat with other users about the game through Facebook Connect. In the figure on the right, note the Details button and the Chat button. The Chat feature is really more like posting and reading comments than true chatting — all handled through Facebook Connect. I've noticed that a lot of this chat is really just team fans talking smack to each other, so make of it what you will.

The app also offers league standing, news, which opens up news articles from other sources, and you can get alerts. Note that alerts cost additional money. The Pro version of this app means that it comes without ads, but alerts are still extra, handled via in-app purchases.

The free version of this app is ad supported, and offers most of the features the Pro version offers.

Best features

The app is designed well, has a very good interface, and is feature-rich.

Worst features

I think they would be well-served by offering more sports, and there's something about paying extra for alerts in an app I've already paid for that rubs me the wrong way, but then you don't have to subscribe to alerts in the first place.

CBS Sports Mobile

Free (ad supported)

CBS Sports Mobile offers you scores, news, team information, schedules, and videos from CBS Sports. Sports covered include the NFL, NCAA football and men's basketball (no coverage of the NCAA women's programs), the NBA, the NHL, MLB, golf, racing, and tennis. I honestly liked this app less than the Fox Sports Mobile app — its interface is clunky and slow, and navigation isn't thought out very well. What it has going for it are colorful graphics, video clips from CBS's extensive coverage, and access to current college polls. Sporting apps are one of those subjective things, and because this is one of the most popular apps on iTunes, I thought it warranted mentioning.

Fantasy Football Cheatsheet '09

$1.99 US

Fantasy sporting leagues are a big deal these days, with football and baseball probably being the most popular. Fantasy Football Cheatsheet '09 is an app that many fantasy footballers will find very useful for drafting their teams and seeing recent stats and results for their players. You can put together multiple draft pick lists, and the app includes some 500 ranked players and 900 total players. It has "up-to-the-minute" player news and injury reports, and includes past and present stats where applicable. Each new season gets a new app, so shop accordingly.

GolfLogix Golf GPS

Free limited download
(Requires in-app purchase of $39.95/year after 24 hours)

Golf GPS devices basically combine a GPS with golf course information to tell you distance information on every hole of the covered golf course. GolfLogix Golf GPS turns your iPhone into such a device, giving you detailed course information on 24,000 golf courses around the world (!) right on your iPhone. With this app, you get distances to layups, hazards, as well as the front, center, and back of every green. You can also use it to keep score, and it even lets you enter in the specific clubs you're using on that day's golfing adventure. The app is a free download, but it requires a $39.95 per year membership after the first 24 hours.

PocketDyno+
$12.99

Don't try this on the street, kids, but PocketDyno+ is like having a full-blown dynamometer in your pocket. Using the iPhone's accelerometer to measure drag racing performance of your vehicle, it can measure real-time Gs, speed, and distance, 0 to 60 MPH (or 100km/h) time, estimated wheel horsepower, reaction time with a simulated drag tree, 60-, 330-, and 1,000-foot times, ¼-mile and ⅛-mile times, and trap speed. It also lets you have multiple vehicle profiles so you can measure and store data for all your cars.

I can't swear for the accuracy but in my limited (track-only) testing, it seemed to do a credible job for a thirteen-dollar app.

Ski and Snow Report from SkiReport.com
Free

If you've ever lived with a skier or snowboarder, you know that they can be obsessive about checking the ski and snow reports for whatever ski resort happens to be close. This app, provided by SkiReport.com, facilitates that obsession by offering quick reports that are frequently updated. It uses your iPhone's GPS to find resorts near you, give you their status in a list, including the snow base for open resorts, and new snow. Tap through and get details like what kind of snow is on the ground, first-hand reports, and how many lifts and trails are open. If you ski or snowboard, you want this app.

15 Travel, Navigation, and Weather

FlightTrack Pro
$9.99 US

This app brings out the geek in me, and I bet it will do the same thing for you. As the name suggests, its main purpose is to track flights, in real time, with updated statuses, or even on a map. How cool is that? In addition, it pushes alerts out to you for changes in flight information and remembers the flights you've entered so you don't have to re-enter them again. The app also offers integration with TripIt to automagically fetch your personal flight itineraries without you having to enter a thing.

Start with the basic features: I've chosen a couple of random flights to monitor, and the app keeps them in a list for me until I delete them. For quick updates, all the basic information I need is right there. For instance, for the three flights I am currently monitoring, I see that all three are en route. I have flight numbers, departure and arrival times, and the departure and destination cities.

If I tap through to one of the flights — in this case, the Sacramento to O'Hare flight in the figure on the left — I'm taken to a screen that has gate numbers, terminals, times . . . Hey, what's this? This flight is going to be early? That little warning popped up just in the nick of time for me to get a nice screenshot of it. You can see the flight information behind the warning pop-up, but it's the warning that's probably the most important thing here. Getting that information pushed to my phone when I'm supposed to pick someone up is a heck of a lot easier than calling the airline or even looking it up on the Web.

The status area in the upper-right corner of this screen rotates through flight status, elevation, and speed. As you all know by now, I'm an information junkie, and I enjoy seeing that sort of data, even if it doesn't help me all that much.

Now, if I want to really geek out, I can tap the Map button at the top of the screen. On that screen, you see a map of the flight path, with the flight path itself drawn in red, as you can see in the figure on the right. You can see where the airplane is, too, along with weather radar so you can know if your loved ones are going to be flying through any kind of serious weather. How cool is that?

Other features include the capability to e-mail flight info directly from the app. The e-mails have the latest flight status (including updated arrival times) and a still from the same map I have below! Alternatively, I could tweet the current flight status through the built-in Twitter support. Lastly, I can see the full itinerary for a flight by tapping it, which takes me to that itinerary in Safari.

This is a very slick app with sophisticated flight-tracking capabilities. If you fly a lot, or if you have colleagues or loved ones who fly a lot, you'll want this app. If $9.99 is more than you want to pay, for $4.99, you can get the regular version of FlightTrack without the push alerts, airport delay notifications, or support for TripIt.

Best features
The push alerts for any kind of flight status change are really helpful, especially with so many late flights these days.

Worst features
You can't see more than one flight at a time on the Map tool, but that's not likely to be something that you need to do very often, anyway.

MobileNavigator North America
$89.99 US

Of the half-dozen or so GPS apps I've tested, the one I prefer is MobileNavigator by Navigon. Granted, I don't think any of the iPhone GPS apps I tested is as good as the GPS system built in to our Acura MDX, but then again, none of the iPhone apps sells for more than $99. And although I can't remember the exact cost of the Acura system, I'm sure it was quite a bit more than $1,000. I also have a Magellan RoadMate pocket-sized GPS that sells for around $100, and I think the MobileNavigator is just as good and possibly better. Plus, I can't help thinking that the RoadMate, which hangs off of the inside of the wind-shield, is a temptation for thieves to break into my car and steal it. Because the iPhone leaves the car when I do, theft is not an issue with an iPhone-based GPS.

One of the things I like best (and that some people hate most) is that unlike some apps, this app doesn't choke when you don't have an EDGE or 3G network signal. Some of the other apps just stop working until you obtain a cellular connection again. As a result of this, the app is huge — 1.5GB — but that's a trade-off I'm willing to make to avoid having my GPS die if I'm in a dead zone.

I find MobileNavigator's user interface a model of efficiency. I had trouble figuring out how to access some of the functions in other GPS apps, but this one makes everything easy to find and use. Because I hate to type on my iPhone keyboard, I love the intelligent address entry system, as shown in the figure on the left. It guesses state, city, and street names as I type them, saving me innumerable keystrokes. I also like the one-tap access to my iPhone contacts, which also saves me taps and keystrokes.

Some iPhone GPS apps don't pronounce street names. MobileNavigator does, and it does a pretty good job with most of them, even the tricky ones.

Perhaps my favorite thing about MobileNavigator is its 3-D Reality View, shown in the figure on the right. It's pleasing to the eye and easy to deci-pher. As you can see, I'm half a mile from an interchange and the screen display makes it really easy for me to determine which lane I need to be in. The map automatically switches between day and night, getting brighter by day and dimmer by night. Nice!

Other useful features include support for landscape and portrait mode, route planning, and optional real-time traffic reporting, known as Traffic Live, which costs an additional $25. I've only had my MobileNavigator for a few days, but so far I think it was a bargain — even though it doesn't always report traffic as accurately as I'd like.

I also like to be able to listen to and control music without leaving MobileNavigator. MobileNavigator automatically resumes navigation after an incoming phone call, another nice touch.

Because $89.99 is a lot to pay for an app, I'd be remiss if I didn't at least mention a much less expensive option that's also quite good. It's called MotionX-GPS Drive, available with 30 days of Live Voice Guidance for just $2.99. You can purchase additional 30-day Live Voice Guidance packages whenever you need them for another $2.99.

Best features

MobileNavigator doesn't need an EDGE or 3G network connection to function, has a great user interface and terrific 3-D maps, and announces street names.

Worst features

It's not cheap. If you also purchase the optional $25 Traffic Live package, it's the most expensive GPS app in the iTunes Store today.

 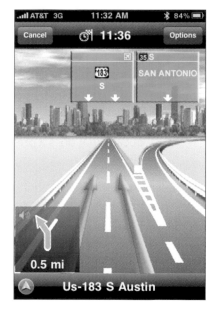

Priceline Hotel Negotiator
Free

Discounted hotels and a video of William Shatner busting his way through a plywood wall? Sign me up! Seriously, what more could an iPhone owner want in an app?

Priceline Hotel Negotiator is a dedicated app for finding hotel-only deals through Priceline's online service. Priceline (`www.priceline.com`) is a discount online travel service that first made its mark by allowing you to name your own price for hotels with a specific star rating in a given area, and then matching that price with a hotel that accepts it. The upside is that you can get some killer hotel deals this way. The tradeoff is that you don't know which hotel you'll end up with, and if you bid too low, you won't be able to make another bid for that star rating and area until the next day.

After that initial approach helped set the site apart, Priceline eventually added airlines, car rentals, cruises, and other forms of travel-related services, and then it eventually also allowed you to browse for set discounted rates for those services.

Hotel Negotiator is, therefore, a subset of what Priceline as a whole offers, and it's being marketed with an extensive campaign fronted by spokesperson William Shatner (you know, *Star Trek*'s original Captain Kirk). That's why his picture is on the app's icon, and why he's kicking things off by busting through that wall. This app allows you to use the Hotel Negotiator service on your iPhone, and the company has done a pretty good job of making an iPhone app that is easy to use.

To start the process, choose the city you're looking to book a room in. I chose Austin because I have some family flying in for the holidays, and I thought it would be cool to kill two birds with one stone. I hope you don't mind. After you choose your city, you're taken to the Negotiator tab, where you can see recent winning bids for hotels at various star rating levels in all the different neighborhoods in the city, as you can see in the figure on the left. You can see the number of stars, the percentage saved in the winning bid, and the specific price.

If you tap one of these items, you're taken to a new screen with dates and a slider that represents how much you're willing to bid. Set your price, tap the Bid Now button — I decided to go aggressive with my bid, as you can see in the figure on the right — and you're taken to a new screen that has all the real details and more information about how the bidding process works. The key to Priceline's bidding system is that you have to pay up front — if your bid is accepted, you are automatically booked (and paid) in the hotel that did the accepting. It's part of why hotels are willing to participate with Priceline on these discounts.

In any event, if you can handle a little risk in finding a hotel room, you aren't likely to find better deals than through Priceline Hotel Negotiator, at least not in my experience.

This app also lets you browse hotels and see their published prices. These are usually the same prices that all the online travel agencies offer, for what it's worth. To see prices this way, tap the Browse tab after you've chosen a city. There you can find a list of popular, mostly nice hotels. You can filter the list by popularity, star rating, or neighborhood, but I wish I could search, too.

Best features

The app is easy to use, and if you can accept some risk in booking your hotel, it's a great way to find a deal.

Worst features

Hotels should be searchable in Browse mode, but they're not.

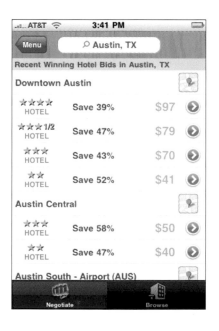
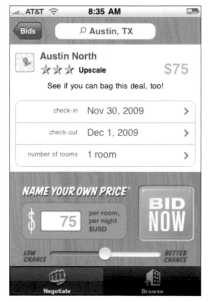

Travel Assistant Pro
$4.99 US

I'm not the most organized of travelers, so I've really enjoyed seeing all the travel-related apps that have come out for the iPhone. Travel Assistant Pro seems like it was made just for me. With this app, I can keep all my itinerary information in my iPhone, and with its built-in support for TripIt and TripIt Pro Web-based travel organizers, I can get that information instantly updated by simply shaking my iPhone. It's just what I need!

The first thing to understand about Travel Assistant Pro is that it's a great app even if you don't have a TripIt account. You can enter complete itineraries (see figure on the left), including flights, trains, cruise information, or other stuff for, say, driving in a car or maybe taking a bus. You can also add taxi or car service plans, car rental reservations, hotel, and other accommodation information, with an Other Event category for something that falls outside those parameters. You can add notes for your trip, and then add contacts for the trip under two sub-tabs, Trip People and Event People.

After I've added all this information, for example, I can e-mail it out directly from the app so that all those things I normally lose track of are with my wife. She likes that.

That's not all, though. Travel Assistant Pro lets me enter my rewards programs broken down by airline, hotel, train, cruise, or car rental, with an Other Travel category, just in case. Better yet, after I enter these the first time, Travel Assistant Pro remembers the information for future trips. That is so what I need! The app also has a Travel Log feature for notes and lists for me to make for packing or shopping or whatever — see the sample list in the figure on the right.

Many screens with important information (rewards program entries, addresses, flight information, and so on) allow you to rotate your iPhone to have that info presented full screen with large letters. It's great for when you need to give your numbers to someone else.

Now, that's all fantastic. It's everything I needed to keep my basic travel information organized and handy. With TripIt or TripIt Pro integration, however, the app becomes even more convenient. With a free TripIt account, you can e-mail any ol' itinerary you've received from a travel agency, airline, hotel, car rental service, and so on, to your TripIt account, and it's available in its entirety on Travel Assistant Pro without you having to enter anything at all.

If something about that itinerary is updated (say your flight is delayed), TripIt lets you know through the app, too. All you have to do is shake your iPhone to sync it with TripIt for the latest information. TripIt is free, whereas TripIt Pro is $69.95 per year. With the Pro version, you also get updated information for such things as gate numbers and baggage claim carousels. You don't need TripIt to use this fantastic app, but if you like the service, the support is a great convenience.

Best features

Being able to get status and other itinerary updates with just a shake of your iPhone (with TripIt) is an awesome feature, and having all my travel-related information with me in one source is so convenient that even I can't lose it.

Worst features

I haven't been able to figure out how to get Travel Assistant Pro to get my baggage from baggage claim, but I'm ever-hopeful.

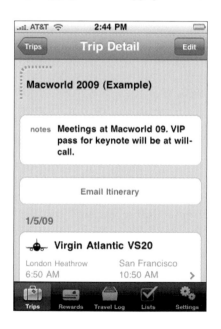
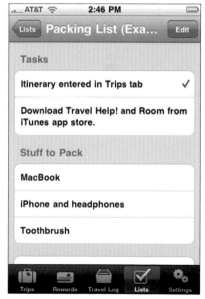

WeatherBug/WeatherBug Elite
$1.99 US

Here's sort of a dirty little secret, so don't tell anyone: I bet I check the outside temperature on my iPhone more than I do anything else. It's true. If I want to know how to dress, I've found that the iPhone is hands-down the fastest way to get outside weather conditions. Your iPhone comes with a handy little app called Weather for getting current conditions and a multiday forecast, but real weather bugs are going to want to check out WeatherBug Elite, a wonderful app for getting the temperature, conditions, forecast (seven day and hourly!), alerts from the National Weather Service, access to live weather cams, cached information for viewing offline, satellite and radar maps . . . the list goes on. I tell you, this is a great weather app.

Check out the figure on the left. It's my home town of Austin, Texas, where it's 48 degrees as I'm writing this. This is the main page for checking out the conditions for cities for which weather conditions are compiled and made available to the public. In addition to temperature, I can get the current conditions, wind direction, wind chill, dew point, and humidity. At the bottom of the screen is today's forecast.

To see a seven-day forecast, tap the arrow in the lower-right corner of the screen in the panel with today's forecast. Each day is presented as a forecast for the daytime and additional forecasts for the evening and night. You can drill down still further by tapping either panel for the hourly forecast (from 6 a.m. to 11 p.m.) for that day. You can also get the seven-day forecast by tapping the Forecast tab in the main navigation bar.

You can watch multiple cities, too. In the Home button at the top of the screen, you can add whatever cities you want and then swipe through them in the other views. The app defaults to your current location if you allow the app to use Location Services on your iPhone. WeatherBug Elite offers both U.S. and international locations, although not all of the services are available outside the U.S.

Next to the Forecast tab is the Maps tab, which you can see in the figures. The app uses Doppler Radar, satellite imagery, and other views, which are pulled through Microsoft Visual Earth, so you can see exactly what's happening and where. At the top of the screen, you find buttons for setting preferences, including which view you want to see, what kind of conditions, and so on. I wish I could show you a dozen screenshots for this app because a lot of these map views are gorgeous. You really need to see them to understand everything this app can show you.

Other features of WeatherBug Elite include a daily weather video from the WeatherBug Web site (www.weatherbug.com) that offers a forecast and weather recap from a weather person. You can find that in the Video tab. It's a national look at U.S. weather, so it's no substitute for your local TV station's weather segment, but you can pull it up on demand, which is handy.

The last tab in this app is the Camera tab, where you can look at the view from weather cameras installed in your watched cities. Just swipe through the current image to move to another live camera view. Note that the last several images from each camera are included, and you can animate them by tapping the Animation button at the top of the screen.

A free version of the app called WeatherBug is available. It's ad supported and doesn't have some features of the Elite app, but it still packs a punch in the weather department.

Best features

This app offers comprehensive weather coverage at your fingertips. It's like having a meteorologist in your pocket!

Worst features

Some international cities listed in the app don't actually have weather stations.

Google Earth
Free

The Google Earth app for iPhone offers users the same amazing satellite views of (most of) the planet as the company's desktop Google Earth map, and I think that's just amazing. Covering "half the world's population" and "a third of the earth's land mass," Google Earth for iPhone lets you spin a globe to pick a spot, and then drill all the way down to a street-view of that location. It's too cool, and you need to try it to believe it. The globe spins, you can turn on access to geo-located Wikipedia articles, and even see geo-located photographs from around the world if you turn on the Panoramio feature.

MapQuest 4 Mobile
Free

Remember MapQuest? It's what you used for online directions before Google Maps came along. Ah, I kid MapQuest, I kid! The company has made a great iPhone app that is especially good at finding local businesses. When you view a map, you see a row of buttons for turning on displays of hotels, restaurants, retail stores, gas stations, coffee shops, and post offices. Just tap each button and get a quick overlay of that category of locations on your map. Tap the location and get more information on or directions to that business. It's pretty darned slick, intuitive, and useful. You can also get turn-by-turn directions, of course, and save locations to My Places.

NOAA National Weather Service
$1.99 US

If you like your weather a little dryer (pun intended) than WeatherBug Elite, NOAA National Weather Service may be the weather app for you. It pulls its data from the National Oceanic and Atmospheric Administration (NOAA) and the National Weather Service, and presents it pretty much as-is. You can get local conditions, forecast, a map view, and radar information, all in a fairly no-nonsense fashion. In addition to the local-condition information, this app also has marine conditions and forecast, including a high-seas forecast. This isn't the prettiest weather app out there, but the information it offers is complete and comprehensive.

Postman
$2.99 US

You know, when you travel, you really should send a postcard to your loved ones to show them you miss them, or at least what they're missing! The Postman app for iPhone allows you to do this with photos you take on your iPhone (there's a library of images, too), and then personalize it just like a postcard. Customize a message, customize the font, or wrap your image with one of several very professional-looking themes. You can write something to your friends on the "back" of the card, and then send it to people via Facebook, Twitter, e-mail, Tumblr, or by posting it on the Web. It's super-easy to use and a lot of fun.

TideApp
Free (ad supported)

If you sail, surf, fish, or swim (or whatever) near coastal waters, check out TideApp for current tide information. The app brings this information from all over the world and includes current conditions and the forecast for both low and high tides during the day. It includes sunrise, sunset, moonrise, and moonset information, too. You can add specific locations to a Favorites tab for quick viewing later, and each location also offers a chart view — you can swipe through these charts for past and future days. Hundreds of locations around the U.S. are offered, and what seems like all the major ports around the world, so have fun!

16 Utilities

Air Mouse Pro
$5.99 US

Air Mouse Pro (also known as Mobile Air Mouse) is a versatile app that can magically transform your iPhone into a wireless remote control system for your Mac or PC. With it, you can control your computer from across the room or even from another room (although that can be difficult if you can't see your computer display). The point is that the remote works from anywhere in your home or office that has Wi-Fi reception.

After you install the free Air Mouse Server software on your Mac or PC, you can control the mouse cursor on your computer screen two different ways: by accelerometer or by trackpad. In accelerometer mode, you press the yellow trigger shown near the top of the figure on the left and then wave your iPhone around in the air. The mouse cursor on your computer screen moves more or less in tandem with your hand. Alas, I found accelerometer mode made it quite difficult to control the cursor accurately; although when it works, this method makes an awesome iPhone demo. I found trackpad mode, in which the top half of your iPhone screen acts like the trackpad on a laptop, much easier to use.

In either mode, you can enlarge the trackpad area by shaking the iPhone from side to side. You can tap the lower-left part of the trackpad to emulate a left mouse button click and the lower-right part to perform a right-click. Rotate your iPhone a quarter turn to use it in landscape mode, which makes it easier to type because the keys on the alphanumeric keyboard (not shown) are bigger.

In addition to the trackpad modes, Air Mouse Pro includes four keyboard layouts. The first layout is the standard iPhone alphanumeric keyboard. The other layouts are a media keyboard with buttons for play, pause, next/fast forward, previous/rewind, and so on; a Web keyboard (shown below on the left); and a programmable remote keyboard with function and arrow keys (shown below on the right).

The coolest thing about Air Mouse Pro is that you can program the buttons on the media and Web keyboards to do what you want for the programs you like. For example, you can program the buttons to work in iTunes, PowerPoint, and DVD Player. Air Mouse Pro automatically detects which program you are using and switches to the button assignments you set for that program.

Using Air Mouse Pro takes a bit of practice. If you're willing to give it a bit of your time, however, you'll be rewarded by being able to control your computer from across the room with Air Mouse Pro, almost as well as you control it using your usual mouse and keyboard.

Best features

Air Mouse Pro turns your iPhone into a totally programmable remote control for your Mac or PC!

Worst features

You have to practice Air Mouse Pro to use it effectively. It also occasionally lags or loses contact with your Mac or PC.

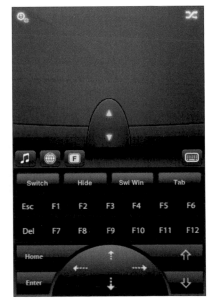

AppBox Pro
$0.99 US

AppBox Pro combines 18 useful apps in one inexpensive package. I was going to say it is the Swiss Army Knife of iPhone apps, but it's more like a Swiss Army Arsenal. The 18 apps (which I'm going to call modules to avoid confusion) are Battery Life, Clinometer (with surface/bubble level), Currency Converter (with 195 currencies), Date Calculator, Days Until (also known as Countdown), Flashlight, Holidays (for 83 countries), Loan Calculator, Periodic Calculator, Price Grab, Random Number Generator, Ruler, Sale Price Calculator, System Info, Tip Calculator, Translator, and Unit Converter, plus direct links to Web apps. You can see the icons for all these modules in the figure on the left.

Two things in particular make this app a winner in my opinion. The first is that after I installed AppBox Pro, I was able to delete nine or ten individual apps from my iPhone. Although it's true that many of the apps AppBox Pro replaced were freebies, it also means I have room for nine or ten other apps on my iPhone.

The second great thing about AppBox Pro is the quality of the modules, which is mostly outstanding. I didn't expect these modules to be as good as or better than stand-alone apps I've seen, but most of them are. For example, there are dozens of flashlight apps that are free or only cost a buck or two. The Flashlight module in AppBox Pro is at least as functional as the best of them. Although the AppBox Pro Unit Converter module isn't as pretty or easy to use as some of the other conversion apps you can get (such as the excellent ConvertBot I raved about in Chapter 2), it has pretty much the same functionality, right down to being able to display only the units I need (such as acres and square feet) and hide units I don't care about (such as hides, roods, rods, and poles).

Some of the AppBox Pro modules aren't particularly beautiful, but all are usable, and they all do what they are supposed to do quite nicely. Check out the Unit Converter shown in the figure on the right. The AppBox Pro Unit Converter module offers pretty much the exact same functionality as the prettier ConvertBot, and for the price, you get a bunch of other modules, too. On the other hand, some of the other modules, such as Clinometer and Battery Life, are almost as handsome as any of the stand-alone apps.

AppBox Pro includes a couple of modules I never would have considered had they been stand-alone apps, even if they were free, such as Loan Calculator and Price Grab. But I found the Loan Calculator, with its A/B comparison mode, quite useful when I was shopping for a car not too long ago. I'm not very math-savvy, so I love the Price Grab module, which lets me compare the prices of any two items and then tells me the cost per unit (ounce, pound, gallon, and so on) for each. I never would have thought to look for an app like Price Grab, but now I use it all the time.

Best features

How can you not love 18 mostly useful app modules for less than a buck? Sure, you won't use them all, but even if you only use a handful, AppBox Pro is a bargain.

Worst features

It doesn't work at all in landscape mode, which means that some Web apps don't work properly (if at all). And the procedure for adding new Web apps could be easier and more intuitive.

GottaGo
$1.99 US

Imagine that you're attending the most boring meeting ever. You know that suddenly remembering you need to be somewhere else will look suspicious. But you wish you had a credible excuse to leave.

The solution is the GottaGo app, which may turn out to be the best two-dollar app you ever bought. Just set its timer, and at the appropriate moment, GottaGo makes it appear that you're receiving a phone call, SMS text message, or MMS multimedia message that looks thoroughly realistic but is actually a fake. This app can definitely get you out of any situation, assuming you don't crack up laughing as I did the first time I tried it.

Start by configuring your Call, SMS, or MMS Settings. The Call Settings screen is shown in the figure on the left; the SMS and MMS Settings screens are pretty much the same. As you can see, I've set up my fake calls to look like they're from my wife Lisa. I used the picture and ringtone I'd see and hear if she were calling me for real, and I selected the wallpaper I'm currently using on my phone to make the fake incoming call look realistic. As you can see in the image on the right, the simulated phone call looks perfect. The Decline and Answer buttons work like the real things, so if you tap the Answer button the translucent in-call button overlay (Mute, Keypad, Speaker, Add Call, Contacts, and Hold) appears, and it looks perfectly realistic as well.

To make the situation even more realistic, you can record audio that plays when you answer your fake call. I recorded my wife saying, "Honey, I've fallen and I can't get up," but I couldn't keep a straight face when I heard it. Now her recording says, "Honey, I'm afraid we had a little incident here at the house." She then pauses long enough for me to say, "OK, do you need me to come home now?" She replies, "Yes, please. And please hurry." If anyone is standing near me they can hear enough of her voice to believe it's really her calling. If I want to enhance the effect, I can tap the Speaker button and everyone in the area can hear her.

GottaGo includes a setting for what is displayed on the screen until the time your fake call or message is due to arrive. One option is a black screen, which makes it look like your iPhone is asleep. If you

choose the Slide to Unlock screen instead — which looks totally realistic, just like everything else in GottaGo — you can make the fake call
or message appear before the appointed time by unlocking the phone.
As soon as you do your fake incoming call or message appears on the
screen.

After you set up the Settings screen(s), you merely set the timer for
between five seconds and 60 minutes, tap the Gotta Go! button, and
you're ready to get out of whatever hateful task awaits you.

GottaGo is simple to set up and looks totally realistic. If you don't
mind being a little deceitful, you can extract yourself gracefully from
almost any situation as long as you don't laugh or get caught.

Best features

Everything about GottaGo is so realistic that even the most eagle-eyed
iPhone enthusiast won't be able to tell you're faking it.

Worst features

The battery display doesn't appear in green as it should on my iPhone
3GS, and it always appears half-full (or half-empty if you're a pessimist).

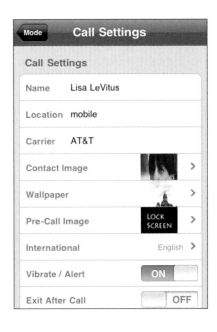

Night Stand
$0.99 US

Simply put, Night Stand is the most attractive and full-featured alarm clock app I've seen (and I've seen quite a few). I know some of you are thinking, "But the iPhone comes with a Clock app that has a built-in alarm clock, so why would I want to spend even a buck on Night Stand?"

I'm glad you asked. Okay, I know you didn't actually ask, but I'm going to tell you anyway. Night Stand is better in almost every way and much better looking than the Clock app's alarm clock.

Let's start with beauty. I find it relaxing to look at the Metanoi theme, which is shown in the figure on the left. The glow pulsates subtly and the second hand (the little purple dot at 3 o'clock) sweeps smoothly around and around. Compare that to the built-in alarm clock app, which doesn't even include a visual clockface. Night Stand, on the other hand, has a lovely visual clock (see the figure on the right) and lets you choose from five other attractive themes designed by Piotr Gajos, who is an Apple Design Award winner.

Beauty is skin deep, though, and I wouldn't recommend this (or any other app) just because it's pretty. I recommend Night Stand because it's pretty *and* — in addition to having almost every feature the built-in alarm clock has — Night Stand has some terrific features the built-in alarm clock doesn't have.

Take screen dimming, for example. The built-in alarm clock doesn't have anything like it. As I said, it doesn't even have a clock face. Night Stand has a really nice dimming feature that's easy to activate or deactivate even when you're half asleep. To dim the clock, you double-tap the screen; to brighten it, you tap once again.

Another nice feature is that you can listen to music from your iPod while you fall asleep at night. Just specify how long you want the music to play before Night Stand fades it out. I happen to like falling asleep with music playing, but I don't like it to play all night. So I think this is an especially sweet feature.

You can adjust the Night Stand snooze setting to let you sleep for 5, 10, 15, or 30 additional minutes. The iPhone's built-in alarm clock has only one default snooze setting, which I think is five minutes.

There's a clever option called Math Puzzles, which forces you to solve a simple math problem — such as "How much is (20 * 8) – 20; choose either 140 or 143" — when you tap the Turn Off button. Night Stand continues to sound the alarm until you tap the correct answer.

If you travel much or work with an office in another time zone, you'll love Night Stand's dual time zone support. One of the themes displays two clocks on screen at once; the other five themes let you swipe a finger across the screen to switch time zones.

Unlike the built-in alarm clock, Night Stand is rotation-aware, so when you turn your iPhone sideways the clock display turns sideways, too. The clock even becomes a little bit larger when in landscape mode.

I saved the best feature for last. The built-in alarm clock can only wake you up to one of your ringtone sounds; with Night Stand, you can pick any song or songs, playlist, or album on your iPod. I'd probably pay a buck for that feature alone.

Best features

Night Stand has too many good features to mention, and many that you won't find in the iPhone's built-in alarm clock.

Worst features

The one thing the built-in alarm clock can do that Night Stand can't is quit the app and still have the alarm go off. It's disappointing that the alarm won't go off after I quit Night Stand, but it's not a deal-breaker for me.

Perfect Web Browser
$3.99 US

The more time you spend surfing the Web, the more you'll like this nifty app. The humbly named Perfect Web Browser is an alternative Web browser that does almost everything Safari can do and does almost all of those things faster than Safari. The number one reason to love Perfect Web Browser, though, is that it offers oodles of features you won't find in Safari.

For example, Perfect Web Browser has tabbed browsing, as shown in the figure on the left. Two-and-a-half tabs are visible in the figure, but you can create as many tabs as you want. To see a tab that is not currently visible, flick the tab bar to the left or right. To hide the tab bar, tap the little blue triangle below the tab bar's lower-left corner.

Perfect Web Browser loads and renders tabs in the background, so while you're reading one page you can have half a dozen (or more) additional pages loading in the background. That means there's no waiting for those pages to load — tap a tab, and that page is already rendered and ready to read.

Furthermore, if you enable the Restore Last Session option, Perfect Web Browser remembers what tabs you have open so that they reopen the next time you launch the app.

Another great option is Web Compression. If you enable this option, most Web pages you visit will appear on screen noticeably faster. Actually, Perfect Web Browser feels faster than Safari, even with Web Compression turned off. Plus, it uses an advanced caching scheme so that subsequent visits to pages load as much as 40% faster.

One of my favorite features is that I can hide and show the address bar at the top of the screen, the toolbar at the bottom of the screen, and — as I mentioned before — the tab bar, each with a single tap. I can also hide them all at once with a single tap and have a completely unobstructed full-screen view, as you can see in the figure on the right.

Notice how the word *button* is highlighted in yellow in the figure on the right? I'm showing off another cool feature of Perfect Web Browser — the capability to search for text within a Web page.

Also visible on the right side of the screen shown in the figure on the right is a gray bar with blue arrows at each end. This feature is called Hyper Scroll, which overlays a real scroll bar on the right side of the page. Just press the red line (near the top in the figure on the right) and drag it to scroll up or down. With Hyper Scroll you can get to the top, bottom, or any place in between quickly and easily.

Other superlative features include an option to clear all cookies when you quit the app, a private browsing mode (meaning no history is created for the pages you visit), a rotation lock to prevent accidental page rotation, and the capability to send a page from Safari to Perfect Web Browser, where it opens in the full-page view.

That last feature is especially welcome because although Perfect Web Browser includes bookmarks, it doesn't import or display your bookmarks from Safari.

The bottom line is that I think Perfect Web Browser is so cool that I removed the Safari icon from my iPhone's Dock and replaced it with Perfect Web Browser.

Best features

Faster Web surfing and tabbed browsing are my favorite features, but full-screen browsing and in-page search are also awesome.

Worst features

Perfect Web Browser doesn't import or display Safari bookmarks.

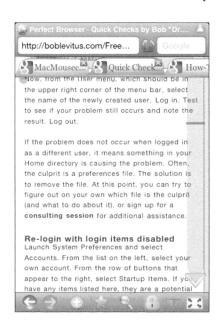

Email 'n Walk
$0.99 US

Email 'n Walk lets you compose and send e-mail while you're on the run (or walk) by using your iPhone's camera to display what's in front of you in a transparent message form. In other words, Email 'n Walk lets you see right through the message as you're typing.

The app description says, "Note: We can't take responsibility for your stupidity, so please don't walk into traffic, off cliffs, or into the middle of gunfights while emailing." That cracks me up.

I'd like it better if Email 'n Walk let me compose and send SMS messages, but it's still a pretty cool way to multi-task, and it only costs a buck.

Flashlight
Free

You won't need Flashlight if you bought AppBox Pro (described earlier in this chapter) because a flashlight is one of its 18 tools. But if AppBox Pro isn't your cup of tea, try Flashlight. It's a flashlight app that offers every feature you could possibly want and then some. You can shine it in red, white, blue, or any other color you choose. You can use it to check that every pixel on your iPhone screen is working. You can even use it as a strobe light.

A flashlight is a handy app to have, and this one is full-featured and free.

iEmoticons — Emoji. Smiley, Emoticon Keyboard
$0.99 US

Some people have never embellished an e-mail, SMS, MMS, or chat message with tiny, colorful, images; other folks would include them in everything they type if they could. If you're one of those in the second group, you'll love iEmoticons — an app that gives you more than 400 little pictures you can insert into anything you type on your iPhone.

The little pictures, often called Emoji or Emoticons, include all the familiar yellow smiley faces, plus hearts, aliens, dining utensils, balls (football, soccer, baseball, and so on), animals, flowers, electronic devices, and many more.

The Emoticons are a little dorky, but if you like dorky things, you can get a lot of them for only a buck.

iHandy Carpenter
$1.99 US

If you do any type of carpentry work, or if you just like carpenter tools, iHandy Carpenter provides five useful carpenter tools — plum bob, surface level, bubble level, protractor, and ruler — in a single app. Just getting those tools makes this app worth having, but the tools are also among the most beautiful iPhone tools you can get. I don't know that I'll ever need them for carpentry purposes, but they were so pretty I bought them anyway.

If you want to see just how nice-looking an app can be, try iHandy Level Free, which is the same bubble level tool found in iHandy Carpenter, but for free.

RedLaser
$1.99 US

Ever been in a store trying to figure out whether something would be less expensive if you bought it on the Internet? If so, you're going to love RedLaser, which scans barcodes and gets you prices for the item using Google Product Search and Amazon.com. It's surprisingly accurate and fairly quick. Although it wasn't great at finding prices for inexpensive items such as food or beverages, it did great with higher-ticket items such as electronic devices, power tools, and almost everything that cost more than $25 at Home Depot.

It's one of a very few apps that has actually *saved* me money.

17 My Ten Favorite Free Apps

Top Free Apps

- Comics
- Concert Vault
- Eliminate Pro
- Google Mobile
- Instapaper Free
- Lose It!
- Now Playing
- Pandora Radio
- reQall
- Skype

Comics
Free

If you read my review in Chapter 1, you can tell that I really love this app. My biggest gripe was that the app didn't have enough comics from "the big guys (such as Marvel and DC Comics)." The app now has more than 150 titles from Marvel Comics, including my all-time favorite, Spider-Man! Many of the titles are classics, including issue #1 of *The Amazing Spider-Man*. Released in 1963 for 12¢, a copy in excellent condition goes for at least $25,000 US today!

I also talk about Guided View in Chapter 1. The figures below show what that looks like on an iPhone screen. On the left is the entire front cover; on the right is the same artwork broken into two panels as they appear on your screen. The top panel on the right appears full screen, and then the "camera" pans slowly downward and to the right to reveal the bottom panel.

The bottom line

If you like comics or graphic novels, you're sure to enjoy this app.

Concert Vault
Free

What I didn't have room to say back in Chapter 9 is that the Concert Vault iPhone app is rockin' awesome (pun intended). But a big part of what makes it so great is that it's linked to a companion Web site called Wolfgang's Concert Vault (www.wolfgangsvault.com).

The companion Web site is fantastic because it is easier to browse and search than the iPhone app, and it allows you to create an unlimited number of playlists featuring songs from different concerts. The iPhone app lets you listen to these playlists but not create them. The figure on the left shows my Todd Rundgren/Utopia playlist, which features tunes from half a dozen different concerts. One final point: the iPhone app lets you add concerts to your "favorites" list, but you can only delete them from the Web site!

On the flip side, the iPhone app is terrific because the user interface is clean and easy to navigate, as you can see in the figure on the right. The app works over WiFi, EDGE, and 3G networks, and the Wolfgang's Concert Vault Web site is barely usable on the iPhone's Web browser.

The bottom line
If you love classic rock music and want to hear exclusive live performances, Concert Vault is just the ticket.

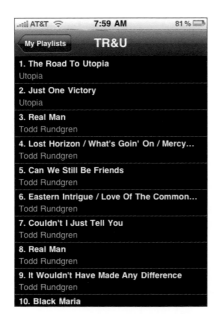

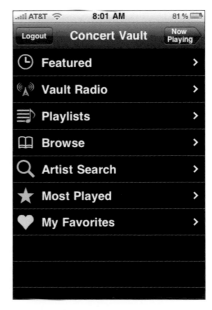

Eliminate Pro

Free

Eliminate Pro, a first-person shooter game, offers two modes of play: offline practice games and multiplayer online games. Offline practice games, which pit you against computer-controlled (actually iPhone-controlled) robots, are challenging and a lot of fun. They don't deplete your energy, which is good. Unfortunately, they don't earn you any credits, either, which is bad.

The multiplayer online games, on the other hand, let you compete against other living people in real time. These games earn you credits based on your performance, and you can use your credits to buy better weapons or armor or additional energy. Better gear helps you play better so you earn more credits per game. But you only get to play a few games before you run out of energy. At that point, you can either use some of your credits to buy more energy, wait a couple of hours for your free recharge, or purchase additional energy using real money (actually, iTunes Store credits). I'm cheap, so I wait for the free recharges, but if you're willing to pay to play, it'll cost you around a buck or two (US) per hour.

The bottom line

Playing hasn't cost me a cent and I'm having a lot of fun. I still have mediocre weapons and armor, and I still pretty much stink, but even so, I dare you to eliminate me. My handle is *levitus*; come and get some. . . .

Good luck.

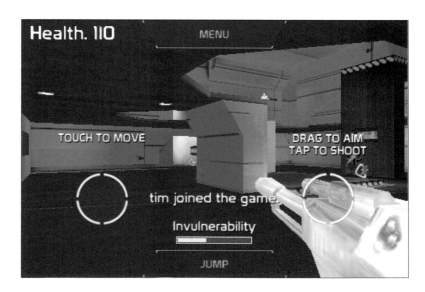

Google Mobile
Free

Let me tell you a couple of the reasons I love this app:

- ✔ **Reason #1:** Its speech-to-text engine is amazingly accurate. I've tried many speech-to-text systems over the years, including continuous voice recognition (dictation) software for PCs and Macs, such as Dragon NaturallySpeaking and MacSpeech, as well as iPhone apps that include ReQall and QuickVoice2Text Email. Google Mobile is as good as or better than all of them.

- ✔ **Reason #2:** If you meet someone who asks how your iPhone works, demonstrate it by pulling yours out, launching Google Mobile, and asking it to search for something on the Web. Then hand it to the person and watch their jaw drop when they see the search results on the screen. Not many apps work as well for an iPhone demo, and that's priceless.

And one last thing: I recently discovered that you can tap the magnifying glass on the left side of the Search field to narrow your search, as shown in the figure on the left (iPhone and Web is the default). When I selected Images and searched for the University of Texas tower at night, the results were even better than the figure on the left in Chapter 12, as you can see in the figure on the right below.

The bottom line
Searching the Web with Google Mobile is better, easier, and more fun than using Safari.

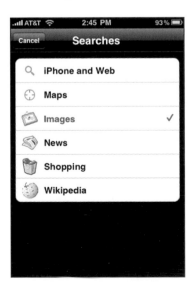
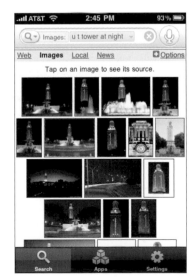

Instapaper Free
Free

As part of my daily ritual, I scan a dozen or more Web sites every morning for articles of interest. I often come across long articles that I'd like to read *if I only had the time*. So I use the handy Instapaper Read Later bookmark I've saved in Safari on my Mac and on my iPhone, which adds the page to my unread items list in Instapaper and lets me get back to work.

Then, when I have down time, I launch Instapaper Free and catch up on my reading. The great part is that I can read one or all of the articles even when there's no network access whatsoever, such as on an airplane, boat, or submarine.

That alone would be worth the price (Ha — it's free!), but Instapaper also has a Graphical Pages setting that I turn off so that only the article's text is captured by Instapaper, as shown in the figure on the left below. If I need to see the graphics, I click the link at the top of the article and the original page appears in Safari, complete with ads, banners, and other graphics, as shown in the figure on the right.

The bottom line

Instapaper Free lets me read lots of Web pages I might not get to read otherwise.

Lose It!
Free

I've struggled with my weight for as long as I can remember. I've tried every diet and exercise program you've ever heard of and I'm on a first-name basis with many of them — like Jenny, Weight, and Body For!

The truth is, I've never found anything as easy as using Lose It! to track the calories I swallow (eat) and burn (exercise). And because my iPhone is always in my pocket, I tend to actually use it a lot more than any diary, notebook, worksheet, or other means of tracking I've ever tried.

I love being able to see at a glance how many calories I could still eat today without going over my budget, as shown in both figures below. On the left is an overview of my day; on the right are the details. As the figure shows, I could eat as many as 669 more calories today without exceeding my budget.

Being able to see that info with just a couple of taps motivates me to stick to the plan much better than anything else I've ever tried.

The bottom line

The more I use the Lose It! app, the better I like it. And the free companion Web site, with stats, charts, and backups of your data, is a nice touch.

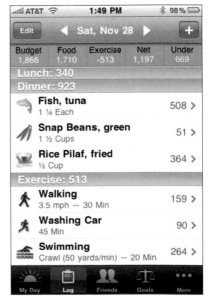

Now Playing
Free

I love movies and I use the Now Playing app all the time, even when I'm not planning a trip to a theatre. What I didn't have the space to tell you back in Chapter 4 is that Now Playing is great for renting DVDs and checking out movies that aren't even out yet.

For example, my family likes to rent DVDs. Because Now Playing has a comprehensive listing of recent and upcoming releases, we can sort by either release date or title. That means we can look at what DVDs came out last Tuesday, as shown in the figure on the left, and decide what we want to see before heading to our local Blockbuster or Redbox. You can also see the same information for Blu-ray discs if you want, but because I'm a Luddite without a Blu-ray player, I have that feature turned off.

Another cool feature is that I can look at movies being released in the coming weeks and months, such as *Avatar*, shown in the figure on the right below. I can watch the trailer (which, by the way, is great) right on my iPhone, or read about it at Amazon (`www.amazon.com`), the Internet Movie Database (`www.imdb.com`), or Wikipedia (`www.wikipedia.org`).

The bottom line

If you like movies, even just a little, Now Playing is a fantastic resource.

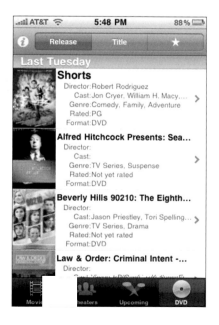

Pandora Radio

Free

I love Pandora, and I listen to it all the time on my iPhone and on the Web (at www.pandora.com). It's the best thing I've ever used to discover new music that I'm almost certain to like. The reason Pandora works so well is something called the Music Genome Project, which performs the Pandora magic behind the scenes. It consists of hundreds of musical attributes or "genes," that together capture the unique and magical essence of a song — its melody, harmony, rhythm, instrumentation, orchestration, arrangement, lyrics, singing, and vocal harmony.

If you're curious about why a particular song was selected to play on a station you created, tap the little icon with the three white lines (shown in the margin) in the upper-right corner of the Now Playing screen (see the figure on the left).

Tap the Song button (the one that doesn't say Artist) and you see a description of the musical characteristics that caused Pandora to play this track. The song in the figure on the left was played on my Byrds/Tom Petty/Beatles channel, which I call "Jangly Guitars."

Just for giggles, the figure on the right shows you the names of some of the Pandora Radio stations I've created for myself.

The bottom line

Want to hear new music you're almost certain to enjoy? Get Pandora Radio.

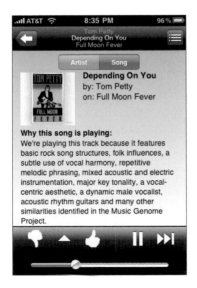

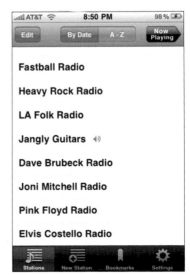

reQall
Free

I think what I like best about reQall is that it remembers things for me with the least possible effort on my part. I say the words and tap the screen a couple of times, and my reminder magically shows up in my e-mail box a few minutes later, as shown in the figure below. And remember how I raved about Google Mobile's speech-to-text recognition a few pages back? reQall isn't as fast, but it's usually just as accurate. And if it's not, the audio recording is enclosed with the e-mail message so that if I can't understand what's written, I can listen to what I actually said.

It's awesome for jotting down quick thoughts at a red light or standing in the checkout line at the grocery store, which is generally when I remember something I need to do but can't easily jot it down.

If I weren't so cheap and had popped for a reQall Pro account, I could even reply to this reminder e-mail with words like *done*, *delete*, *pending*, or *help*.

The bottom line

reQall is free and incredibly useful. I can't think of a single reason not to love it. I love it so much that it's one of the sixteen icons on my home screen.

Subject: **Reminder for Nov 28, 2009 7:00 PM: Buy Lisa some flowers tonight.**
From: reQall <reqall@reqall.com>
Date: November 28, 2009 9:15:09 PM CST
To: Bob LeVitus
Reply-To: reQall <post@reqallmail.com>
▶ 🖉 1 Attachment, 27.4 KB (Save ▾) (Quick Look)

reQall reminder:
Buy Lisa some flowers tonight.
Edit this item

You can control or turn off reminder emails on the reQall Settings page.
You can invite your friends to try reQall.
If you're a reQall Pro user you can reply to this email to tell reQall how to mark this item.
Use a one-word reply at the top of the content area: done, delete, pending or help.

www.reqall.com ◀)) ▶ ◯—————— ◀ ▶

Skype
Free

It's easy to explain why Skype is among my favorite apps — I'm cheap and it saves me a ton of dough. As I mentioned in Chapter 13, I use a SkypeIn phone number for my consulting business. This has several advantages over a traditional business landline:

- ✔ It's much less expensive — using Skype costs me around $70 a year versus around $70 a month for the personal landline I still have in my home office.
- ✔ Because of the way Skype works, my SkypeIn line rings in my office, my Senior Agent-in-Charge's office, and the office of any other agent who is logged in. And, by the way, we all live in different parts of the U.S.
- ✔ I can manage our SkypeIn line right from my iPhone, as shown in the image on the left below.
- ✔ I can see at a glance whether I have business voice mail messages by checking the badge on the Skype icon (which says 6 in the icon shown in the margin).
- ✔ I can listen to business voice mail messages on my iPhone if I choose to. My staff sees the same messages in their Skype apps in Virginia, Minnesota, or wherever else they happen to be.

The bottom line
The app is free and offers numerous advantages to my business. And Skype services are a bargain compared to AT&T. What's not to like?

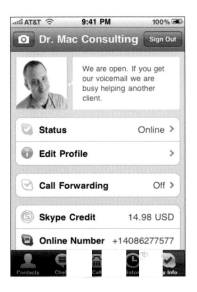

18 My Ten Favorite Paid Apps

Top Paid Apps

- GottaGo
- iEmoticons — Emoji. Smiley, Emoticon Keyboard
- Jaadu VNC
- MusicID with Lyrics
- OldBooth Premium
- Pastie
- QuickVoice2Text Email (PRO Recorder)
- RedLaser
- Reel Director
- Simplify Music 2

GottaGo
$1.99 US

Okay, faking an urgent phone call or text message *is* kind of sleazy and dishonest. So I use GottaGo only in emergencies. Like when a public relations person overstays her welcome (you know who you are), or a meeting drags on and on but nothing is being accomplished.

Nobody has busted me or even looked suspicious the few times I've actually used it. But it has gotten me out of several situations I desperately wanted to get out of.

A GottaGo fake text message is easy to set up and looks totally realistic, as shown in the figure on the left. The figure on the right shows how convincing an SMS text message looks on your screen.

The bottom line

Okay, it may be just a little sleazy or dishonest, but I've gotta tell you, it works like a charm. If you ever need to extract yourself from an unpleasant situation, you gotta get GottaGo.

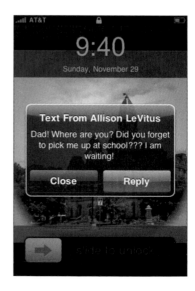

iEmoticons — Emoji. Smiley, Emoticon Keyboard
$0.99 US

When I discuss this app in Chapter 16, I don't have the space to show you what the Emoji emoticons look like. In the figure on the left below, you can see roughly ten percent of the little emoticons available for you to use in text and e-mail messages. In the figure on the right, you can see what they look like when you actually use them. To switch from the alphanumeric keyboard to the Emoji icons, you tap the little globe icon in the lower-left corner. Tap one of the icons on its right — the clock, smiley face, flower, bell, and so on — to reveal different sets of icons.

I like to use emoticons to create rebus puzzles for my wife, as shown in the figure on the right below. Can you figure out what it says? (The answer appears above the figure, in the section called "The bottom line.")

Okay, they really don't save me time or effort or make my life easier in any way, and it would be a stretch to call them artistic, but a friend got my wife into using them, and I couldn't resist. They're corny, but still kind of fun.

The bottom line

If you can stomach such things, Emoji icons are a great way to spice up otherwise boring text or e-mail messages.

Answer: The rebus in the figure on the right below says: "Honey, I love you bunches and bunches. Please call me tonight. Love and kisses."

Jaadu VNC
$24.99 US

Say I'm out to dinner with my wife when my iPhone begins to vibrate in my pocket. I take a peek at the screen surreptitiously and see an urgent text message from my editor:

> *Chapter 18 is missing and drop-deadline is in less than an hour! Please say you can send me the final draft of it right now. If you can't, our geese will be fricasseed.*

Even if I ran out the restaurant door that very second, I couldn't get home in time to save our ganders. But it's no problem with Jaadu VNC on my iPhone. I launch it and, in seconds, I'm in control of my desktop Mac at home, commanding Microsoft Word to send the file to my editor as an attachment, as shown in the figure on the left below. My Mail program launches automatically and creates a message with the file enclosed. I quickly type a subject line and then click the Send Message button, as shown in the figure on the right below.

Crisis averted. Time elapsed between urgent text message and clicking Send Message: Under 3 minutes.

The bottom line

Jaadu VNC has saved my bacon (and my goose) more times than I care to count. It may seem expensive, but I've tried other iPhone virtual network computing (VNC) apps, and none is as reliable or elegantly designed as Jaadu VNC.

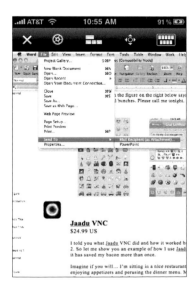
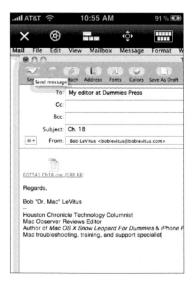

MusicID with Lyrics
$2.99 US

In Chapter 9, I say pretty much all there is to say about MusicID with Lyrics. Simply put, nothing I've tried comes close to this app when it comes to identifying songs by hearing a snippet. And nothing else I've tried (at least not at this point in time) also provides lyrics for most of the songs it identifies. It works better than its better-known competitor, Shazam Encore, and costs less to boot. Let me mention some of the obscure songs it identified correctly for me and one feature I don't discuss in Chapter 9.

The obscure songs it successfully identified, in addition to those shown in the figure on the left below, included "Witch Doctor" by the Chipmunks, "What a Difference a Day Makes" by Dinah Washington, "On An Island" by David Gilmour, "Court and Spark" by Herbie Hancock, "Chick Habit" by April March, "Bohemian Rhapsody" by the California Guitar Trio, "Tarkus" by Emerson, Lake & Palmer, and "Prelude/Nothin' to Hide" by Spirit.

The feature I didn't have room for in Chapter 9 is called Similar Songs. Tap the Similar Songs button on any Song Info screen to see suggestions — like songs similar to King Crimson's "In the Court of the Crimson King" that are shown in the figure on the right below.

The bottom line

An iPhone app that listens to music and tells you the song title and artist's name is one of the coolest things I've ever seen.

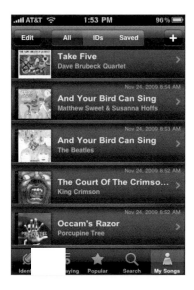

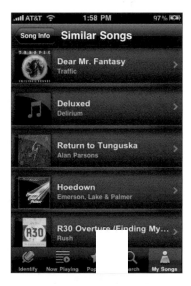

OldBooth Premium
$0.99 US

OldBooth Premium is just plain fun. In Chapter 10, I show a bunch of pictures of my wife and me that I defaced (pun intended) in OldBooth Premium. So now let me tell you why I love it and show you a little of the app.

As I explain in Chapter 10, you start by selecting a male or female mask from the nearly 60 that are included. The figure on the left shows a couple of each sex that you haven't seen yet.

Then you choose a picture to deface. In the figure on the right, I've used a picture of me with my face rotated upside down so that you can better see how the mask and my picture interact. To rotate the picture, you merely drag on the ring visible in the figure on the right. You can adjust the brightness of the mask, the picture, or both to get a realistic effect.

The bottom line

Every iPhone owner I've ever defaced with OldBooth Premium — and I've defaced a lot of 'em — ends up buying the app. It really is that much fun.

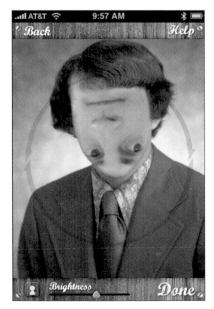

Pastie
$2.99 US

I love my iPhone, but my rather large fingers aren't designed for typing on those tiny keys. So any app that saves me from typing is an app I can appreciate. Pastie saves me a boatload of keystrokes every time I use it, and I appreciate that a lot.

As I mention in Chapter 11, Pastie lets you save commonly used expressions and messages and then paste them into an e-mail or SMS message or copy them to the clipboard. You can see some of my "pasties" in the figure on the left below. If I tap the first one, the Messages app opens and the text contained in the first pastie ("I'm in a meeting…") appears on the iPhone clipboard so that I can paste it into a new text message (or messages) to send to whomever I choose.

The fourth pastie in that list has a contact, my wife, associated with it. When I tap it, the Messages app opens, but in this case, the message recipient is selected automatically, so all I have to do is paste the text and tap Send. Two taps.

Finally, if I tap the sixth pastie, a new mail message appears with the text already inserted, as shown in the figure on the right below.

The bottom line

The Pastie app saves me countless keystrokes every day. It's a winner. Don't tell the developer, but it's worth more than three bucks to me.

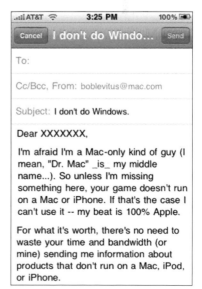

QuickVoice2Text Email (PRO Recorder)
$0.99 US

As I've said before, my fat fingers aren't exactly made for typing on an iPhone keyboard. So the more keystrokes an app can save me, the more I love the app. That's why I love QuickVoice2Text Email so much.

Wonder how many keystrokes I save when I use it for a typical e-mail message? Say I'm in traffic and realize that I'm going to be late for dinner. I pull into a parking lot, launch QuickVoice2Text Email, tap the Record button, and say, "Honey, I'm running late. Please put the coals on the BBQ. Thank you. I'll be home at 8:00. Love you." I tap the Email Recording as Text button, as shown in the figure on the left below, tap my wife's e-mail address, and tap Send.

Elapsed time: Around one minute. Taps required: Fewer than 10. Keystrokes avoided: At least 99 (the number of characters in my message).

A few minutes later, my wife receives my message with the exact words I spoke (in quotes, no less), plus the audio file in case my voice wasn't translated to text properly. The message she received is shown in the figure on the right below.

The bottom line

This 99¢ app saved me several minutes and kept me from having to type at least 99 characters. You have to love that, and I do.

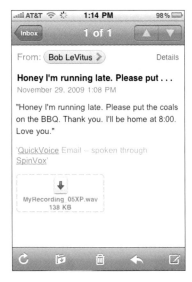

RedLaser
$1.99 US

In Chapter 16, I tell you how awesome I think RedLaser is. But because a picture is worth a thousand words, and every picture tells a story, let me now *show* you why I love RedLaser so very much. . . .

I was cruising the aisles recently at a big-box retailer when I came upon a very cool digital camera that had an LCD display on its front as well as its back, making it great for self-portraits and such. I launched RedLaser and aimed my iPhone at the barcode on the box, as you can see in the figure on the left below. As soon as I held the iPhone still enough with the barcode aligned (which, as you can see by the blurry barcode, wasn't easy for me), RedLaser beeped to tell me it had successfully scanned the item. A few seconds later, the results, as shown in the figure on the right, appeared on my screen. After comparing the price in the store to what it cost online, I could see that I could save more than $50 by buying the camera online.

The bottom line

RedLaser costs less than $2. Using it this one time saved me more than $50. And that, gentle reader, is why RedLaser is one of my very favorite apps and, like the reQall app I discuss in Chapter 11, has earned one of the 16 spots on my home screen.

Reel Director
$7.99 US

I never thought a day would come when I could actually shoot a movie with my iPhone. And I *really* never thought I'd see an app that let me edit the video I shot; re-order, trim and split clips; add transitions, opening titles, and closing credits; and even apply the Ken Burns effect to still photos to simulate motion.

That's all changed with Reel Director. The editing interface is great. You can drag clips in the timeline, as shown in the figure on the left below. You can trim clips, too, so don't be afraid to keep the camera rolling. When you shoot, make sure your scene has adequate light. The video you shoot with your iPhone is noticeably darker than still photos.

You can't change the font size for titles, so make sure your title fits. My original title for the movie shown in both figures below was, "Spider-Man vs. The Dummies Man," but the text ran off the screen. To make it fit, I changed it to the shorter title you can see.

The bottom line

If you have an iPhone 3GS and enjoy making movies, you'll love having Reel Director on your iPhone. Before I got Reel Director, I hardly ever shot video with my iPhone. These days, I love making movies with my iPhone, and I think you will, too.

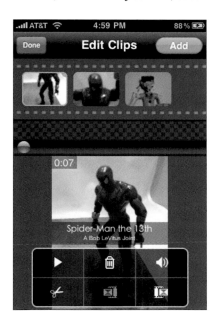

Simplify Music 2
$5.99 US

Here's the deal: With all the other stuff I have on my 32GB iPhone 3GS — the apps, videos, and photos — I only have enough space left for around 2,500 songs. The problem is that I have more than 6,000 songs in my iTunes library, and I have a terrible time deciding which songs should be synced with my iPhone and which songs should be left behind.

For a mere $5.99, Simplify Music 2 makes it a total non-issue. As long as iTunes and the free Simplify Media server are running on my computer at home, I have access to all my playlists (some of which can be seen in the figure on the left below) and all 6,017 songs in my iTunes library.

But the coolest part is that two of my friends also have iTunes and the Simplify Media server running, as shown in the figure on the right, so I also have access to my friend Darrel's (aka "dd" in the figure) 17,000+ songs and my friend Homer's 11,000 songs!

The bottom line

Simplify Music 2 gives me access to all 6,017 songs in my iTunes library, plus tens of thousands of songs in my friends' iTunes libraries. That rocks, and it's worth a lot more than $5.99 to me!

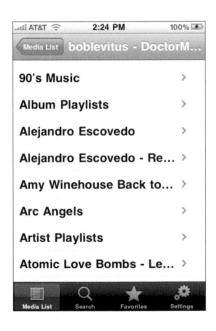

19 Ten Things That Make Your iPhone Better

I spend a lot of time looking at iPhone and iPod peripherals and accessories as Reviews Director for the Mac Observer (www.macobserver.com) and for my other writing gigs. In this chapter, I try to encapsulate everything I've learned by testing hundreds of products. Rest assured that the products I recommend in these pages are the ones I consider the very best in their categories.

Batteries

Juice Pack Air: $80 US
Richard Solo 1800: $70 US
Kensington Travel Battery Pack and Charger: $70 US

If you hate when your iPhone runs out of juice in the middle of an important e-mail, movie, or game, you may want to invest in one or more external rechargeable batteries. The Juice Pack Air by Mophie is like a battery backpack for your iPhone. As you can see in the photo, it is almost unnoticeable and adds very little weight or bulk. It appears to be nothing more than a protective case, but it can come close to doubling your iPhone's battery life.

The Richard Solo 1800 is the Swiss Army Knife of external batteries, with a built-in laser pointer and flashlight plus a hard-shell case.

Finally, I love the cleverly designed Kensington Travel Battery Pack and Charger, with its built-in dock connector and flip-out USB dongle. It's great for travel because it has no cables to pack or lose. And its protective cap flips open and acts as a kickstand, making it perfect for hands-free movie viewing on a tray table and a great choice for long trips.

Photo courtesy of Mophie

Bluetooth Headsets

Jawbone PRIME: $130 US
Griffin SmartTalk: $100 US
Cardo S-2: $70 US

I've tested many Bluetooth headsets for hands-free calling with my iPhone. These three stand out as truly exceptional:

- ✔ **Jawbone PRIME:** The Jawbone PRIME headset from Aliph has outstanding military-grade noise elimination that suppresses ambient noise — such as traffic, helicopters, or the wind when you're driving with the top down — better than any other Bluetooth headset I've ever tested. Furthermore, it's comfortable, gorgeous, and available in seven cleverly-named colors including Frankly Scarlet, Going Platinum, Lilac You Mean It, and Drop Me a Lime. Jawbone Prime is somewhat expensive, but worth it if you need to make phone calls from noisy environments.

  Photo courtesy of Aliph

- ✔ **SmartTalk Bluetooth:** SmartTalk Bluetooth from Griffin Technologies has noise cancellation that's good, although not quite as good as the Jawbone Prime, and is also quite comfortable. It isn't nearly as handsome as the Jawbone Prime, at least not in my opinion, but it does have a feature the Jawbone does not — a human voice that confirms every operation.

- ✔ **Cardo S-2:** The Cardo S-2 headset is not only the least expensive option, but it's the only stereo Bluetooth headset I've liked enough to recommend. It's bulkier than the others and doesn't suppress noise as well as the others. (I don't think it has any noise suppression circuitry whatsoever.) But it is the only one that offers stereo, making it the best (if not the only) choice for listening to music or playing games.

Car Audio Adapter/Charger

Monster Cable iCarPlay iPod Cassette Adapter: $20 US
Belkin TuneBase Direct with Hands Free: $70 US
Griffin iTrip Auto SmartScan: $80 US
RadTech AutoPower: $10–$17 US

A car audio adapter enables you to listen to music on your iPhone through your car stereo system. Of the three main types, here are my favorites:

Photo courtesy of Belkin

✔ **Auxiliary input:** If you have a car stereo system that includes a 3.5mm auxiliary input jack, you can buy a cable at Radio Shack for less than $10 and simply plug one end into the car stereo's input jack and the other end into your iPhone's headphone jack. This setup offers the best possible sound quality but doesn't recharge your iPhone. A nice (if pricey) solution is the Belkin TuneBase Direct with Hands Free, as shown here. It plugs into your car's 12v lighter outlet and charges your iPhone while also allowing you to use it for hands-free phone calls.

✔ **Cassette adapter:** If your car stereo includes a cassette tape player, this is an excellent choice — it's inexpensive, it sounds better than an FM transmitter, and it's small and easy to conceal if you feel the need. The one I like best and currently use is the Monster Cable iCarPlay.

✔ **FM transmitter:** This type of car adapter broadcasts your iPhone audio over FM radio. Plug it into your iPhone, tune your car radio to an unused frequency, and the music from your iPhone comes out of your car stereo speakers. Sound quality ranges from decent to horrid and can change from minute-to-minute as you drive. An FM transmitter would be my last choice; but if your car stereo doesn't have a cassette player or auxiliary input jack, it may be your only option. If so, the Griffin iTrip Auto SmartScan is the best of the bunch.

One last thing: Even if you don't want to listen to your iPhone in the car, you may want to recharge it. If so, I recommend the RadTech AutoPower Vehicle Socket USB charger, available with one or two USB ports.

Clarifi Macro Lens

$35 US

Clarifi from Griffin Technologies is a one-trick pony, and it's only for the iPhone 3G. That said, it's a great pony, it adds a great feature to your iPhone, and it's integrated with a very nice hard shell case.

The one trick? The Clarifi case includes a built-in lens that lets you shoot macro and close-up photos in finer detail and with more accurate color. It also improves the accuracy of apps that read bar codes, such as RedLaser (see Chapters 16 and 18). Without Clarifi, your iPhone requires you to be back at least 18 inches from your subject so the camera can focus; with Clarifi, you can shoot from as close as 4 inches.

Photo courtesy of Griffin Technologies

The lens slides into the durable polycarbonate hard shell case, which is available in black or white. A nice touch is that the bottom third of the case slides off, so it's easier to use your iPhone in devices with an iPhone dock than it is with a lot of other cases.

Home Speakers

Logitech Rechargeable Speaker S315i: $130 US
iHome iP9BR Clock Radio for iPhone and iPod: $100 US
Audioengine 2: $200

If you want to listen to music around the house, you need a decent set of speakers. Lots of good iPhone speaker systems are available at prices ranging from less than $100 to thousands of dollars. The three I've picked for this section are each notable for at least one unique feature.

- **Logitech Rechargeable Speaker S315i:** This relatively compact system offers extremely good sound for its size. It only weighs a couple of pounds, so it's easy to pick up and move to wherever you happen to be. And it's rechargeable, so you can listen to music for up to 20 hours without plugging it in.

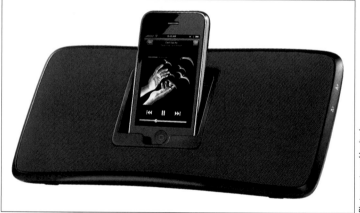

Photo courtesy of Logitech

- **iHome iP9BR Clock Radio:** This system for iPhone and iPod is unique because of just what its name implies — it's a clock radio that can use your iPhone as an audio source. It recharges your iPhone and lets you choose the song or playlist you want to wake up to. Other features include dual alarms, programmable snooze times, a remote control, and AM/FM radio. I really and truly love mine.

- **Audioengine 2:** These self-powered desktop speakers aren't really iPhone speakers at all — they're designed to work with any audio device, including your computer. The reason they're included here is that they are, simply put, the best $200 speakers I have ever heard. And believe me, I've heard a lot. Enough said.

MovieWedge Flexible Stand
$10 US

MovieWedge has to be one of the cleverest gadgets I've ever seen. It's a flexible stand for your iPhone, but it works just as well for an iPod, or almost any other small handheld electronic device. It looks like a tiny beanbag chair with a little lip across its front side to secure your iPhone (or other device), as shown in the picture. It's covered in soft microsuede and, unlike many iPhone stands and docks, it lets you adjust your iPhone to almost any angle for convenient hands-free viewing.

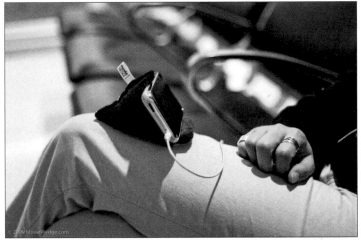

Photo courtesy of MovieWedge

It's great for watching movies and works almost anywhere (even on your knee, as you can see). It works with almost all protective cases and costs less than $10.

How can you not love that?

Protective Cases

iFrogz Luxe and Frosted Luxe: $35 US
RadTech ARC: $15 US
iSkin solo FX and FX Special Edition: $33 and $35

The iPhone is surprisingly resistant to scratches and dings, but I still feel better with something protecting mine. I've tested close to 100 of 'em; here are three I recommend without hesitation:

- **iFrogz Luxe and Frosted Luxe:** I love the iFrogz Luxe and Frosted Luxe cases. And I can't count the number of friends and colleagues who love theirs. The Luxe has a beautiful metallic finish that feels great and makes your iPhone a bit less slippery. The Frosted Luxe is semi-transparent but feels just as nice to the touch. The Luxe comes in Royal Blue, Red Ruby, Thick Black, Medium Magenta, and several other colors; the Frosted Luxe is available in clear, lime, pink, purple, or turquoise. Everyone I know loves these ultra-thin, lightweight cases, and I'm sure you will, too.

- **RadTech ARC:** The RadTech ARC is almost exactly the same as the iFrogz Luxe but sells for half the price. The difference is that iFrogz offers more colors, prettier colors, and the Frosted variation. The ARC has the same metallic finish and feels good to the touch but comes in only black, silver, blue, or red.

- **iSkin solo FX:** I really love the iSkin solo FX (shown here) and solo FX Special Edition. Made of a soft, semi-stretchy, jelly-like material, they look great, feel great, and, unlike the iFrogz and RadTech offerings, include a screen protector. They provide better protection than the iFrogz or RadTech offerings, and the Special Edition is treated with Microban antimicrobial protection, to inhibit the growth of stains and bacteria.

Photo courtesy of iSkin

Screen Protection

invisibleSHIELD for iPhone: Full body coverage — $25 US
Front coverage only — $15 US
Back coverage only — $19 US
RadTech ClearCal 2-pack: $10–$13 US
Case-Mate Full Face Privacy Screen: $20 US

Regardless of whether you use a case with your iPhone, you may want to protect its screen. If you bought one of the iSkin cases I recommend earlier, you're already protected. For everyone else, here are some suggestions:

- ✔ **invisibleSHIELD:** invisibleSHIELD for iPhone is a clear, virtually indestructible film that protects your iPhone from scratches and scuffs. The precision-cut film applies directly to your iPhone and is probably the most durable protection available. The film had its origins in the military, which used it to protect helicopter blades from dust, dirt, and debris. If you choose the full body coverage invisibleSHIELD, you won't need a case (although the cases described in the previous section offer better protection against drops and impacts).

- ✔ **ClearCal:** RadTech ClearCal screen protectors are available for the whole front of your iPhone or only the display. They're available in anti-glare, clear, and mirrored finishes and are the least expensive option; you get two protectors for about $13.

- ✔ **Case-Mate Privacy Screen Pro:** The Case-Mate Privacy Screen Pro covers the whole front of your iPhone and, in addition to providing protection, it prevents anyone who isn't directly in front of the screen from seeing what's on it. Alas, if they're behind you looking over your shoulder, you're out of luck.

Travel Speakers

Livespeakr: $80 US
iMainGo2: $40 US
Altec-Lansing Orbit MP3: $50 US

I like to have music available at all times, and I don't like earphones if
I can avoid them. So I've tested lots of travel speakers over the years.
You can't go wrong with any of these:

- ✔ **Livespeakr:** This is the most expensive travel speaker of the
  bunch, but it's also the best-sounding and the only one with
  at least a semblance of stereo
  sound. It's rechargeable, has
  a cool iPhone cradle that
  rotates, has an integrated
  stand that's great for watching video (as shown), and
  includes a nifty velour
  carrying bag.

Photo courtesy of Livespeakr

- ✔ **iMainGo:** This is a combination iPhone case and high-
  performance speaker. In my 5-star (out of 5) review of the
  original iMainGo, I said,
  "With its reasonable
  price tag, tiny size,
  huge sound, and quality
  construction, iMainGo
  is without a doubt the
  best ultra-portable iPod
  speaker system I've
  seen to date. Or, as my
  18-year old daughter
  puts it, 'That thing
  is soooo tight!'" The
  iMainGo2 sounds better
  than the original and
  costs $20 less.

Photo courtesy of Portable Sound Laboratories

- ✔ **Orbit:** The Altec-Lansing Orbit MP3 is smaller than the others,
  but still sounds great. It runs for days on three AAA batteries,
  has a nice little protective case, and has wrap-around cable
  storage.

DUMMIES.COM®

How-to?
How Easy.

From hooking up a modem to cooking up a casserole, knitting a scarf to navigating an iPod, you can trust Dummies.com to show you how to get things done the easy way.

Visit us at Dummies.com

Wired Headsets

Klipsch Image S4i In-Ear Headset with Mic and Three-Button Remote: $100 US
Scosche IDR350m Increased Dynamic Range earphones with tapLINE
control: $55 US
iFrogz EarPollution Plugz with Mic: $20 US

There's no nice way to put it — the white headset that comes with the
iPhone stinks. It's uncomfortable and sounds mediocre at best. Here
are some replacement headsets at several price points.

The Klipsch Image S4i In-Ear Headset with Mic and Three-Button
Remote is the best-sounding iPhone headset I've tried to date. They
reproduce sound accurately, are very comfortable even for extended
wear, and come with three different ear tip sizes, an ear tip cleaning
tool, a carrying pouch, and a clothing clip. If you can afford these
babies, you won't be disappointed.

Scosche IDR350m Increased
Dynamic Range earphones with
tapLINE control are roughly half
the price of the Klipsch but sound
almost as good and are almost as
comfortable. No pouch or clothing clip, but you do get snap-on
covers in six colors.

Finally, the iFrogz EarPollution
Plugz with Mic don't sound quite
as good as either the Scosche or
Klipsch headsets. But they only
cost $20, sound noticeably better
than the stock Apple headset, and
are available in five vibrant colors
as well as silver (shown here).

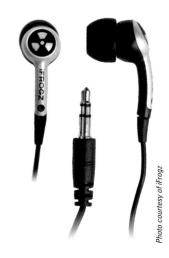

Photo courtesy of iFrogz